GOD SO LOVES THE WORLD

THE IMMATURITY OF WORLD CHRISTIANITY

A. J. van der Bent

ORBIS BOOKS
Maryknoll, New York 10545

To Eliane, Elisabeth,
Vincent, and Christopher

The Catholic Foreign Mission Society of America (Maryknoll) recruits and trains people for overseas missionary service. Through Orbis Books Maryknoll aims to foster the international dialogue that is essential to mission. The books published, however, reflect the opinions of their authors and are not meant to represent the official position of the society.

Library of Congress Cataloging in Publication Data

Van der Bent, Ans Joachim.
  God so loves the world.

  Includes bibliographical references.
  1. Christianity—20th century.   I. Title.
BR121.2.V333 1979   270.8'2   79-4470
ISBN 0-88344-159-4

CONTENTS

FOREWORD

This book raises more questions than it answers. Indeed, it faces with realism, anger, and longing questions on which it is exceedingly difficult to find anything at all to say. Dostoyevsky found that the lonely cry of one anguished child threatened us all with an abyss of tortured meaninglessness. What can we adequately say or do in the face of the Calcuttas of this world? Ans van der Bent has felt obliged to put his Christian faith and understanding to the test of facing up to some of those areas of human anguish, helplessness, and distortion that call in question all our hopes, all our faith, and all our organization and effort. In so doing he has done something profoundly Christian, profoundly theological, and profoundly human. It is Christian because he is always asking what does the tradition of the life and death of Jesus Christ say to us in our dilemmas, our hopes, and our despairs? It is theological because he is always asking how does God speak to us in the midst of our world as it now is, and what question does our world put to our faith in God. It is human because he is always trying to see more clearly what men and women are actually suffering and how, in the churches and as human beings, we are really responding to that suffering and that actuality.

Thus the book is very disturbing because of the penetration of its insights and the uncomfortable realism of its questions. It is also very frustrating for the incompleteness of much of its analysis and for the lack of balance of much of its presentation. But the situation is so disturbing that it can only be witnessed to effectively by a passionate lack of balance. And analyses can scarcely be completed when one is obliged to call in question most of the taken-for-granted analyses and reactions that are habitually used in ecumenical and church circles. A troubling perception of reality can be conveyed, at least as a beginning, only through a troubled and troublingly imperfect awareness of imperfection and trouble. Much of the strength of this book, out of which, under God, some real healing and hope may come, lies in the degree to which Ans van der Bent is truly troubled by, and a true part of, all the troubling things he sees.

I think that he has perceived and is trying to show us that the Christian ecumenical movement is still not ready to be truly ecumenical in the ways which are offered it according to the realities of our world and of the reality of God revealed in Christ through the Spirit. This is the "immaturity of world Christianity" to which his subtitle refers. It is an immaturity and a failure in open perception that embraces all of us, or certainly all of our institutions and churches, so that the criticisms of this book are not written from any standpoint of superiority. Rather it is that the sins and shortcomings of us all need not have dominion over us. But in order to receive this freedom we must also perceive and accept the judgment upon us. This is the judgment of God, which is to be perceived through facing the realities of poverty, anguish, and failure in the world and by facing also the inadequacy and the insensitivity of our responses to these realities.

This book draws our attention to something which my own studies and reflections, from the Humanum studies onward, have been forcing upon me. This is that many churches and, especially, many manifestations of the ecumenical movement, have been ostensibly reacting against many of the features of western cultural imperialism and the narrow optimisms of western technological humanism. Yet to a baffling degree we remain trapped in these presuppositions— even those of us from non-western cultures who are the most (apparently) fierce leaders of this reaction. We uncritically assume the presuppositions of the western nineteenth-century doctrine of progress through science, technology, and liberalism (or else through science, technology, and the errors of liberalism corrected by Marxism). Our Christianity has to be fitted into this. Thus we mistakenly assume that a search for solutions is the same thing as a response to salvation. (See further, my article "Nairobi and the Truly Ecumenical," *Ecumenical Review* 28, no. 3, July 1976.)

We also assume that the latest methods for seeking these solutions are the decisive criteria for serving God and humanity. God can no doubt cope with this. But many men and women suffer from our determination to make our latest criteria of service and of solutions normative for everybody. Thus there is an odd imperialism and colonialism of service and concern, and service and concern continue to be expressed in ways that are calculated to preserve the dominance of those expressing concern and offering service. This, I think, is one of the very important, although deeply disturbing and confusing, insights that run all through this book. And it is something with which the Christian ecumenical movement must come to terms if it is to be part of enabling Christians to serve the Gospel that constitutes them in the world in which they now live.

It should perhaps be added that none of these considerations is intended to reinforce any desire to withdraw from service and concern or any tendency to go back on Christian involvement in the conflict, uncertainties, and struggles of the world. One of the further strengths of this book is that Ans van der Bent is seeking to struggle both with the limitations of Christian ecumenical involvement and concern and with the demands for further and newly ordered involvement and concern to which these very limitations point. Precisely because our basic concern and our fundamental source of hope lie not with the solutions of human beings but with the salvation of God, we are obliged to follow this God along the way of Jesus into the deepest possible wrestling with what men and women actually suffer and with what men and women can realistically hope, celebrate, enjoy, and endure. Hence the detailed discussion of ideologies in this book and the repeated assertion of "the urgency of opting for a consistent, practicable, and coherent ideology" (see page 70 and following pages). Christians must think out what the situation is, what it requires of them, and how they may practically respond to it, with a proper self-awareness of the presuppositions they are using for their analysis and their decisions.

One of the major items on the unfinished agenda posed by this book would certainly be to carry this discussion about a "consistent, practicable, and coherent ideology" further. How do we combine a proper awareness of our individual and collective helplessness and inadequacy with a properly resolute program to attempt what needs to be done or, at least, what can be done? I think it is the argument of the book, which also seems to me to make realistic good sense, that the way to greater maturity lies precisely through wrestling together with dilemmas like this and not indulging in pretence either about our inadequacies or about the demands upon us. We have, in fact, to learn how to live sustained by faith rather than by the righteousness and efficacy of our works. It is by such faith that we shall be set free to offer appropriate and life-sustaining works.

Much, therefore, is left for further clarification and more detailed working out by this book. It is clear, for example, and admitted by the author, that the three theological theses he raises in his concluding chapter are selective, inadequate, and partial. But what is also clear is that the discussion launched here must go on and the questions raised must be faced, either by an extension of the means and arguments which the author indicates or else by better ones that do even more justice to the realities confronted here. Any self-righteous hurling aside of the questionings documented in Ans van der Bent's argument would be a sad betrayal of the journey on which the ecumenical movement has so far come and a terrible confirmation that, in its organized aspects, the ecumenical movement has finally and definitely become more interested in its own identity than in the task for God, men and women, the world, and the churches out of which it sprang.

Moreover, to neglect or to reject the passionate searchings of this book would be to turn our backs on a great source of hope. For to face the judgment upon us, and our helplessness and inadequacies for the tasks of love and of justice that confront us, and to do this with realism and without despair is itself to be open to the Resurrection. In this way we can receive something of the power and promise of the Resurrection in the midst of the world's sufferings and of our failures to find effective ways of caring and responding. So we can be set free to be part of a caring, a responding, and a failing, which can also be part of suffering, part of hope in suffering, and part of celebration that points beyond suffering.

I believe that there are life-giving glimpses in this book of the same possibilities of life out of death, hope out of despair, and celebration out of suffering that were glimpsed also by those of us who worked on the Humanum Studies of the World Council of Churches. In sharing these glimpses I believe we were also sharing glimpses that have been always central to the Christian tradition, the Christian Gospel, and their authentic contribution to hope for all people.

As I come to the end of this Foreword and its poor attempt to support and commend a participation in the arguments which this book presents to all concerned with the ecumenical movement, I therefore take the liberty of inserting a quotation from the speech presenting the final report of the Humanum Studies to the Central Committee of the World Council of Churches at its meeting in West Berlin in August 1974. (See the following quotation from *Humanum Studies, 1969–1975: A Collection of Documents,* Geneva: World Council of Churches, 1975, p. 94 ff.)

We believe that the God whom we praise (and the way in which He calls us to praise him) does not take us away from the realities which threaten and which challenge us. So we do not find it easy to speak of Resurrection. At the moment, wherever we turn, whether to the combat against racism or the struggle with sexism, to the striving for development or the attempts to give a human direction to science and technology, to the fight for human rights or the attempts at political liberation, we do not find victory. Rather we find struggle and we see many in the various struggles facing, if not defeat, at least deep suffering and frustration. Indeed, we ourselves see problems rather than solutions, and struggles rather than established achievements.

Yet we felt that what we glimpsed and do glimpse in the praise of God makes us very positive in and towards these problems and these struggles. To be able to put together the sort of report we are submitting to you is to know something about the Resurrection. [I would here insert in the quotation the remark that to be able to write the sort of book we have here is likewise to know something about the Resurrection.] The reality of human situations and human sufferings requires that we speak of anguish. The realities of the churches (or, perhaps, their unreality and involvement in so much that is past and that is oppressive) demand that we speak of repentance. But we are also free to speak of the praise of God, and we know him and his praise in and through these other realities. This is to know already something of the Resurrection. The Christ whom we must know in our human frustrations, inadequacies and struggles, as well as in our inadequate and so often unresponsive churches, must be the Christ incarnate *and crucified.* But to know that this Christ is with us, is still with us and will always be with us is to know the risen Christ. To discover occasions of hope, of praise and of love; to be able to wait with some expectation even when there is nothing hopeful to expect; to be able to endure without breaking—or even to glimpse the possibility that brokenness is not the last word; to see, from time to time, that it is the *dis*figured Christ who is the *trans*figured

Christ—all this is to know the Resurrection, both as a reality now and as a real promise which will surely be realized. But the anguish of all of us forbids us to speak lightly or easily of Resurrection. We know more about, and we are called to learn more about, incarnation, embodiment, involvement and crucifixion. But this is the way of Resurrection, of Praise and of Glory.

Ans van der Bent here offers us important help in moving along this way.

DAVID E. JENKINS

William Temple Foundation
Manchester, United Kingdom

INTRODUCTION

This book is about world Christianity and the twentieth-century ecumenical movement. My approach to these themes is neither impartial nor apologetic nor destructively critical. I have written the following pages as an eager candidate for world citizenship and as a Christian sharing Saint Paul's insight that "the whole created universe groans in all parts and is to be freed from the shackles of mortality to enter upon the liberty and the splendor of the children of God" (Rom. 8:21–23). With many other fellow human beings I ardently await the coming of God's kingdom. The Sermon on the Mount (Matt. 5:3–16) and the Last Judgment of the Son of Man (Matt. 25:31–46) are two biblical *leitmotifs* of the succeeding chapters. For some strange and inexplicable reasons these two texts have never made the headlines of contemporary Christianity.

The book is nourished further by a very personal experience. Two years ago I had the privilege of traveling widely through Asia and of discovering with my five senses the so-called Fourth World. I spent a few days in Calcutta, the most populated city of India, the largest suppurating ulcer of Asia, and a mirror of global disaster. Calcutta accuses and condemns civilized humanity. It defies Christianity, all world religions, and contemporary secular ideologies. Calcutta unmasks the weakness and shallowness of any religious belief; it resists all charity and relief work; it demythologizes the myth of progress and development, and mocks the most penetrating socio-political theories. People in Calcutta, in the *favelas* of Rio de Janeiro, in the crowded country of Bangladesh, in the slums of Addis Ababa and Nairobi, in the black ghettos of Johannesburg, in the deserts of the Sahel, and many millions more in a great number of countries and cities make up the Fourth World. I shall use the term "Fourth World" at certain points to indicate chronically underdeveloped nations with disastrously low standards of living and hardly any hope of improving even minimally the most basic conditions of human life. Failure to listen and to respond to the harsh and awful cries of all the wretched of the earth will certainly lead world Christianity into a limbo of obsolescence and irrelevance.

Calcutta's population is made up of an almost equal number of Hindus and Muslims and minorities of Buddhists, Christians, Jains, and Sikhs. For several years the World Council of Churches has been to the fore in seeking contacts with representatives of other world religions. It has created a Secretariat on Dialogue with People of Living Faiths and Ideologies, sponsored various bilateral conversations, and participated in multireligious meetings on a world scale. This achievement should not be minimized, for the world religions had never faced each other before. Yet a closer investigation is needed as to whether a common religious desire to pool available resources, to share responsibilities, and to strive together toward a wider community are not in fact a pious glossing over of Calcutta's most grave and perplexing dilemmas. Well-formulated religious statements on the renewal of society, on common goodwill, on world justice and world peace, can be insipid and superficial. The Calcuttas of this world expose many common spiritual and moralizing formulations of community as artificial, idolatrous, and inhuman.

This book also deals with the traditional themes of Christianity as an absolute religion and the Christian doctrine of the history of salvation. The notion of one absolute religion, still so greatly cherished in the West, is useless in situations in which the human mind no longer functions and all search for the truth has come to an end. Engaging in apologetics and proving the absolute truth and value of the Christian faith may still make sense in advanced and prosperous western societies, but defending the uniqueness of the Bible's revelation in the steadily underdeveloping world is a hopeless, Sisyphean task! For several centuries theologies of world history have flourished in the West and been adopted in the East. God's plan of salvation has been meticulously analyzed and evaluated by many prominent Christian scholars. Today ecumenically minded Christians extend the frontiers of God's kingdom and speak of the "indigenization of the Gospel" and "salvation outside the church." But the Calcutta-type pieces still do not fit into the theological mosaic of salvation history. It is not only impossible to believe that people dying a premature and miserable death will be properly cared for in heaven but it is also unacceptable to state that "non-Christians" *may* have a chance to be saved. The Christian doctrinal understanding of the history of redemption has led into a cul-de-sac and no eminent theologian has so far shown the way out.

A chapter on socialist ideologies will show why we have deliberately chosen the subtitle "The Immaturity of World Christianity." Christian social ethics has hardly begun to cope with the crucial problem of understanding the nature and function of an ideology. Contemporary Christianity, I am convinced, will not advance and gain greater maturity and relevance until it is able to state that in many countries of this world a more definite shape of society can and must be ideologically defined and realized in practice. Hammering out a human ideology and praying for the speedy coming of the kingdom of God are closely interrelated. Authentic Christian identity depends in no small measure on the joyous affirmation that God needs many socialists and communists, irrespective of their errors, weaknesses, and failures, to make the impact of the new heaven and the new earth known to all those who yearn for justice and peace.

Finally, I will focus on fresh insights, unexpected options, and very new hopes in contemporary Christianity as it faces God's world with the widest expectations. The churches can discover new ways of being more intimately present in this world, embracing humanity in each place and all places through the unconditional love of Jesus Christ. The more Christians everywhere are drawn to the crucified Lord, the more they see that all people on earth are equally drawn to him and the more they share in his liberation of all helpless, frustrated, and confused men and women. At the same time I would like to point out that the few theological themes in the last three chapters are treated in a purposely eclectic, one-sided, and vulnerable way. They should be considered as exclamations which need to be changed and developed into sentences. World Christianity is sometimes better served, I believe, by partial and disturbing discernments than by all-round and comforting consensus statements. Christian theology can be awkward and lacking in credibility when it veils the heart of the Gospel by a seemingly sound and all-applicable trinitarian doctrine, instead of confidently accepting God's own foolish and vulnerable ways of dealing with his infinitely precious creation. In this respect, too, a greater maturity of worldwide orientated Christianity is needed.

1

CONTEMPORARY WORLD
CHRISTIANITY

Up-to-date theological dictionaries, handbooks, and general or religious encyclopedias provide information about the nature of Christianity, the history of its definitions, major traditional doctrinal issues, the development of absolute claims, the various ecclesiological concepts and liturgical practices, and the attempts to overcome church divisions through the twentieth-century ecumenical movement. Some reference works and general articles on Christianity also include the history of Christian missions, refer to the encounter with non-Christian religions, and discuss the impact of secularization on the Christian religion. Curiously enough, practically none of the essays mentions the process whereby Christianity was institutionalized or gives any space to a description of the organized structures of the Christian churches.

When we consult statistics giving the estimated membership of the principal religions of the world, we learn that, out of a total world population of 4 billion people, almost 1 billion are Christians. In terms of organizations, agencies, and capital funds, there is no doubt that world Christianity, and in particular the churches in Europe and North America, exercise far more power, and are much more ingenious in effective communication and influential in massive service than the existing institutions of all the other world religious bodies put together. Although in a clear minority, organized Christianity employs more executive and specialized staff than the Jewish, Muslim, Hindu, and Buddhist communities, and the Communist parties of the world combined. No statistics are available giving the total annual expenditure of all Christian churches. But it is an unquestionable fact that more than three-quarters of the world population, classified as "non-Christians," are beggars in comparison with the one quarter classified as God's people who have billions of dollars at their disposal for all sorts of religious purposes.

Before dealing with the extraordinary growth, the incredible variety, the spectacular spread, and the undiminished strength of countless Christian institutions—whether administrative, theological, educational, charitable, or of social service—and drawing any conclusions from this account, I would like to raise some critical questions about the present predicament of Christianity. A brief survey of some recent reinterpretations and re-evaluations of the Christian religion will enable us, I believe, to situate the universal church more appropriately vis-à-vis (and not in the midst of) this multireligious and secular modern world.

The End of Conventional Christianity

A considerable number of contemporary theologians are convinced that Christianity finds itself today in a transitional phase, with all the obscurities and uncertainties that inevitably accompany such a transition. Many of the age-old traditional forms of the Christian religion have become obsolete and untenable, they claim. An antiquated Christianity presents all churches and their members throughout the world with a common task of casting Christian faith and life in new forms. Many theologians believe that this will have to be done in such ways that in the emerging world of the future the Gospel will continue to be a divine force contributing to the building of a new world and to the coming of God's kingdom among all people. A work by W. H. van de Pol bears the title *The End of Conventional Christianity*. The author teaches Protestant theology at the Catholic University of Nijmegen in the Netherlands, and this book may be regarded as a prototype of much current theological reflection. The Dutch theologian supposes that the spiritual and religious uneasiness of today is due to the fact that conventional Christianity, as it existed from the first days of the church, is now approaching its final, convulsive end. "The word 'conventional,' " he writes:

is derived from the Latin verb *convenire*. This means to come together, to speak together, to agree. . . . When people agree on something or other and conduct themselves accordingly, such conduct slowly develops into custom. What in certain communities has been agreed upon will almost unconsciously determine and dominate the conduct of all those who belong to that community. In the long run, this will result in a conventional conduct and in conventional viewpoints, attitudes, motives, norms and judgments.[1]

All kinds of philosophical, psychological, and cultural trappings have been woven into conventional Christianity since the time of the church Fathers. The weave is so complex that it is now quite impossible to say what is authentic and what is not. But one thing is certain for Dr. van de Pol: Christian thinking is undergoing the most radical change since the time of Christ, resulting in general religious unrest, the collapse of conventional Christianity, and mass defections from it. In the light of this thesis he examines the effects that modern physical sciences, Freudian psychology, and recent scriptural exegetics have had on traditional Christian theories of God, humanity, and the world. In doing so, he summarizes Christian thinking from Galileo to Harvey Cox, from Darwin to the death-of-God theologians and comes to the conclusion that the traditional theories are completely undermined. Especially three giants among modern theologians—Barth, Bultmann, and Tillich—have prepared the way for the present crisis in belief in God and closed a theological era that now definitely belongs to the past. Their influence, the author argues, will continue to make itself felt. With them "we have now arrived at the post-ecumenical era in which the solution will present itself against the background of a new and responsible belief in God."[2]

The trouble with van de Pol's elaborate study as with so many other similar critical theological treatises recently published is that they assume that conventional Christianity has been and can again become unconventional. This presupposition is contradicted and refuted by the historical facts. The word "conventional," points, as has been rightly indicated, to the conduct and customs of a community. Conventional Christian viewpoints, motives, and norms include the basic notions that God is deeply concerned with the lot of his people, that the church exists as it celebrates the Word and the

sacraments, that the Christian community is under the holy obligation to fulfill its prophetic, priestly, and pastoral roles in this world,
that the "non-Christian" world is destined to be incorporated into
God's visible communion with his people, and that all these notions
must be constantly re-examined and reappraised. From this it can
only follow that conventionality, expressed in these modes of thinking and action, belongs to the essence of institutional Christianity.
There can be no marriage between a conventionally organized
church and a radically conceived unconventionality.

Late twentieth-century theologians are certainly right to contend
that God has been more and more excluded from the scientific
explanation of natural, historical, and cultural phenomena and has
come to stand outside the practice of human living in work and
recreation. Fascinated by the unprecedented advance of technology
and science, human thinking and striving have indeed become
world-centered. This human life is nothing more than the span
between birth and death. Modern men and women find it ever more
difficult to conceive of a world outside this one, of an existence after
death in another world. Surely contemporary religious teachers
must insist that a legitimate and authentic faith in God begins with
God and develops through God's salvific action in and by Jesus
Christ (Karl Barth), that belief in the message of salvation, the
kerygma, is a gift, an act on the part of God (Rudolf Bultmann), and
that faith in God must be expressed in forms other than theism and
supranaturalism (Paul Tillich). Yet all this new theological wisdom
does not really come to grips with the problematic nature of conventional Christianity; it cannot adequately explain the causes, characteristics, and consequences of widespread religious indifference and
the emptiness of Christian buildings. The problem we are facing is
not the question of conventionality versus unconventionality, but
the degrees and limits of the church's conventionality. Conventional
Christianity has not come to an end; on the contrary, in spite of its
apparent unpopularity and decline, it will very likely continue to
assert its power and influence for a long time to come.

Dr. van de Pol distinguishes between three groups of Christians.
The first group tries "to conquer the present unrest by clinging to .
old, traditional teachings and practices." A second broad middle
group is dedicated to an *aggiornamento* of the old Christianity, at-

tempting to find a better expression of the Christian faith and to live out that faith in the changed and changing world. The third group of Christians sees "sharp contrasts between conventional Christianity, which in its view is radically obsolete, and the manner in which man can and must be a Christian in the future."[3]

This third group speaks of Christianity without religion and sometimes even of Christian atheism. Phenomenologically valid though the distinction among the three categories of Christians may be, it does not help us, I am afraid, to answer the disturbing questions whether Christianity, by nature conventional, is able to recognize its captivity to the mores and standards of affluent consumer societies and to what extent it can disassociate itself from the reliable functioning of its structures, built to guarantee visible results that can be universally tabulated. No amount of theological reflection on an "orientation toward a new future" and on a "new and responsible belief in God" helps us to unravel the complex weave of western capitalist and secular values and the Christian Gospel. As long as the cultural domination of the churches in many countries is not radically challenged and as long as these churches actually claim to act as interpreter and champion of the needs and welfare of all humanity, the acceptance of the lordship of Christ will logically mean happiness, security, and contentment of all people and not disruption, risk, and discontent at many levels.

Throughout this book we shall see that this problem is not solved by theologizing about the end of conventional Christianity in a seemingly existential and universal context but in fact in a western world of security and abundance that allows room for ever new academic speculations. Only when rich churches and rich theologies —theologies developed by not starving, not poor, not exploited, and not prematurely dying theologians—look in each other's mirror and mutually detect their poverty, their transitory existence, and their false claims of enduring worldwide relevance, is there hope that some remedy against inveterate conventionality will be found.

Charismatic Movements

Some encyclopedic articles on contemporary Christianity mention recent Christian renewal movements springing up all over the world as the result of new transcendental experiences. Church history has always been filled with the records of battles between proponents of the free emotional expression of the Holy Spirit and the rigid organizational structures of worship, life, and thought. But whereas in the past, tongues, prophecy, ecstasy, the new birth of the Spirit, and charismatic gifts were left to the "sects," in recent years these terms and experiences have come to be a part of the life of all Christian traditions. Roman Catholics, Lutherans, Episcopalians are gathered by the thousands for charismatic renewal. Congregations are turned upside down by parishioners who have suddenly begun to speak in tongues. The rapid growth of the charismatic movement is particularly noticeable in the so-called younger churches as they possess an inexhaustible life of piety and are often closer than the mother churches to the charismatic roots of the Gospel. For many Christians the charismatics contribute to the experience of a one-sided type of a theologized, intellectually diluted Christianity, filling it again with new expressions of ancient spiritual contents. Quite a few other Christians, however, have greeted the renewal movements with scepticism, fear, and even open hostility. Holiness and Pentecostal groups are charged with being narrow in their interests, anti-intellectual, and excessively self-righteous. Theologians seriously question their excessive preoccupation with the Third Person of the Trinity.

I do not wish to discuss here whether the new charismatics are a divisive threat to the institutional church or a vital agent of inner renewal, able to breathe life into its structures. What concerns us here is the fact that even charismatic revivals are in danger of unsuspectingly falling victim to the same trap of accommodation that grips larger parent churches. Although baptism of the Spirit brings with it a vision of the whole person, of the wholeness of human life, and a sense of urgency for mission in society, the perception of the realm of redemption is strangely narrow. The cultural captivity of the churches equally captivates charismatic revivals within those churches. There is no deep awareness that a renewal of individuals without the redemption of the whole society in which they live is hardly sufficient for the renewal of the church, which is Christ's body broken and given for the life of the world. In contrast to the past, current charismatic movements look largely middle-class, riding on the tides of upward economic and social mobility. Their cultural capitulation is expressed in an emphasis on private virtue, an accompanying social acquiescence, and an inner sense of well-being. Enshrining these values, the spiritual communities are well on the way to becoming comfortable and contented with their socio-economic environment. They do not contest the larger society but draw upon and enjoy its cultural values and call them Christian.

Our short analysis of a few major trends and interpretations of contemporary Christianity leads us to the conclusion that the process of institutionalization of religion, which started long ago, cannot be reversed or halted even in our days. In a worldwide context not only Christianity but all other religions have been able to survive for two thousand years and more because their faiths were embedded in mundane structures. Religious institutions help people even today to unify their individual experiences by drawing together all the loose ends of the manifold human crises and perplexities into one meaningful whole. They give human beings a sense of being an integral part of a long heritage from which most of the convictions, values, and actions of today have arrived. Institutional religion and organized ideology provide for people's need of recognition and self-esteem, function as an authority over moral decisions, help them to overcome or to sublimate human injustices and to justify their social commitments. Especially in the present era of rapid socio-political change, religious and secular institutions give individual persons a sense of continuity and stability in the midst of flux. They thus serve effectively to define the identity, mission, and activity of their members over against all other institutions.

Having ascertained this, we cannot but further admit that among the world religions Christianity is among the first to have grave difficulty in recognizing and using responsibly the forms of influence and power which it has possessed for centuries, simply because of the sheer magnitude and range of its impressive and excellently running operations in every corner of the globe. Unable to resist considerable pressures to integrate individuals and societies in its definitions and structures, the church continues to carry out many of its programs for its own institutional self-interest and thus seems to respond to the deepest religious and psychological needs of most of its believers. To be sure, profound differences in doctrine, worship, individual and social ethics still separate Christendom from all the other world religions. But a still deeper cleft exists between, on the one hand, the thousands of Christian councils, commissions, committees, societies, congregations, departments, secretariats, many of them meeting in fireproof and air-conditioned buildings and all ceaselessly working for the spiritual well-being of the Christian communities, their credible witness, and their generous service to the world, and, on the other hand, other religious and nonreligious communities, which are far less experienced in appointing committees and task forces and which invest considerably less money in projects of relief and aid and in the production of literature in many different modern languages.

In order to understand more fully the churches' powerful control over ecclesiastical, missionary, and charitable matters, it is necessary, I think, to spend a moment pondering over their almost uncountable assets and annual expenditures. The following brief survey may seem to be theologically and spiritually irrelevant and a wilful obscuring of the pertinence of the Christian faith and its worldwide expression. In spite of that, I accept the risk of approaching conventional Christianity in a really unconventional way. I believe that my argument on the previous pages is only strengthened by making known something of the staggering wealth of the churches and pointing to the extraordinary variety of Christian institutions. My statement on page 4 that almost 1 billion people are Christians needs to be modified. There are far more uncommitted than committed Christians. Perhaps we can speak of 300 million active Christians. Perhaps there are even less obedient and active followers of Jesus Christ. Keeping this fact in mind, we should be even more baffled by the inexhaustible material and human resources assuring the well-being and expansion of conventional Christianity.

The Power of Christian Establishments

Among all the churches the Roman Catholic church, as is well known, is the largest and most hierarchically organized. The Roman Curia is made up of numerous congregations, secretariats, and councils. I mention here only the Secretary of State, the Congregation for the Doctrine of the Faith, the Secretariat for Christian Unity, and the Commission on Justice and Peace. The Congregation of Propaganda Fide—it is now also called by a non-Latin name, the Congregation for the Evangelization of Peoples—is so large that it manages its own financial affairs. The Vatican State is a true Goliath in economic terms, administering several billions of dollars, using sixteen banks, and paying its Cardinals like international directors. Few records are kept in this vast financial domain; certainly none are open to public scrutiny.

Episcopal conferences in many countries are organized in various departments, committees, and divisions. The National Conference of Catholic Bishops in the United States, the Bishops' Conference in the Federal Republic of Germany, and the dioceses in these two countries, for instance, have enormous donations and funds at their disposal. Caritas Internationalis (the International Conference of Catholic Charities) figures among the largest Catholic relief organizations. Mention should also be made of two comparatively recent and big West German agencies that were born after World War II: Misereor and Adveniat. Together they collect more than 50 million dollars annually. Misereor dedicates its efforts to Africa; Adveniat "specializes" in Latin America.[4]

Alfred Balk, a feature editor of *Saturday Review,* in his book *The Religion Business,* quotes from a statement made by Eugene C. Blake, former General Secretary of the World Council of Churches:

When one remembers that churches pay no inheritance tax (churches do not die), that churches may own and operate business and be exempt from the 52 per cent corporate income-tax, and that real property used for church purposes is tax exempt, it is not unreasonable to prophesy that with reasonably prudent management, the churches ought to be able to control the whole economy of the nation within the predictable future.

A few pages further on Balk adds:

According to a study sponsored by Americans United for Separation of Church and State the religious organizations' "visible assets"—land and buildings of all kinds—now have a value of at least $79.5 billion: almost double the combined assets of the country's five largest industrial corporations. Of this treasure approximately $44.5 billion worth is held by the Roman Catholic Church. These estimates have not been challenged.[5]

The book contains much more information on ecclesiastical endeavors and on many other financial figures. I just record here another few data. Episcopalians have sharply criticized the spending of more money on the towering Washington, D.C., cathedral, which already has cost over 30 million dollars and still requires more than an equal sum to complete. Little precise information is available on the large financial resources of Protestant missionary societies in many countries, but it is known that Church World Service, a department for aid of the National Council of Churches of Christ in the U.S.A., annually administers 35 million dollars, while Christian Aid, the British counterpart, has a yearly amount of 10 million dollars at its disposal. The World Council of Churches in Geneva receives every year approximately 45 million dollars for programs and projects proposed by member churches and church-related agencies in six continents. The Council functions as a broker and a channel.

All major national denominations occupy large buildings and numerous offices, tend to all kinds of administrative and internal tasks, and run an impressive number of urgent programs. Whether Angelican, Methodist, Presbyterian, Congregational, in Great Britain or in the United States, whether Lutheran in Germany or in Scandinavia, whether Reformed in other European countries—churches in the Third World have carefully copied sophisticated western institutional working patterns—all national headquarters are top-heavy, labor-intensive, and cumbersome organizations, made up of boards, councils, commissions, etc., with a great variety of aims and functions: church information, press, publishing, worship, mission, unity, education, lay training, welfare and social programs, liturgy, evangelism, church membership, pension funds, homeland and world ministries, stewardship, chaplaincies, doctrinal matters, ecclesiastical courts, church statistics. Huge sums of money are given and invested in all these enterprises and concerns. The total annual income of the United Methodist Church in the United States for 1972, for instance, amounted to $833.9 million. Its property and other assets were calculated at $6.2 billion. The Church of England annual budget amounts to nearly 30 million pounds. Although the assets and income of the Eastern Orthodox churches are not officially known, their great wealth is unquestionable.

It is further difficult to estimate the total cost of editing, printing, and distributing several thousands of denominational journals, national, regional, and local serial publications, church records, minutes, and yearbooks. More than sixty thousand new Christian books and paperbacks are annually published by religious publishing houses in the western hemisphere. As most books have a minimum impression of two thousand copies, a total of at least 120 million Christian books are printed and sold each year. Only a portion of the total Christian publishing business, running into many millions of dollars, could in itself more than adequately feed the undernourished populations of several countries in Asia and Africa. A partial sale of ecclesiastical assets and land would significantly raise the living standards of several more underdeveloped nations. As a result, millions of people could lead a more secure and dignified life, reaching perhaps an average age of forty to fifty instead of twenty-five years or less.

A number of objections will likely be raised to such a crude tabulating of the churches treasures and expenditures. Cathedrals and chapels are, after all, liabilities and not assets. They have to be maintained and cannot be sold. Even in the richest countries with a large population of Christians, such as the United States and the Federal Republic of Germany, national denominational headquarters and local parishes are nowadays in financial difficulty. Their budgets are increasingly more limited and sometimes are even being severely cut back. The churches have to make painful decisions about options and priorities. If sixty thousand religious titles and well over five thousand journals are annually published in the West, a similar amount of literature is produced in all natural and other sciences. As the Christian churches are deeply embedded in the spectacular industrial growth and technological advance of the last hundred years, a thorough reassessment and drastic overhauling of complicated and expensive church structures can hardly be carried out without undermining the visible and solid foundations of the Christian communities. It is unthinkable that the Vatican should move out of its impressive historical buildings in Rome; the Interchurch Building at 475 Riverside Drive in New York cannot be abandoned if millions of dollars have to be administered every year.

Obvious and valid though all these and other arguments are, I am still as puzzled as before by the fact that 300 million Christians own more establishments and run more organizations than the establishments and organizations of all other religious and ideological communities combined. For several years we have heard that the rich countries are becoming still richer and the poor countries still poorer. The same is true in the religious realm. And precisely in this realm, matters of exploitation, injustice, inequality, and incredibility of the Gospel must be judged even more severely than in the secular realm. I said that conventional Christianity has not come to an end. I now wish to add that talking about the end of conventional Christianity is deceitful and hypocritical. Because of its material power and wealth, which greatly affect its spirituality and theology, the church at large has remained more or less the same phenomenon of domination and prestige, not accepting other religious communities on an equal footing in bilateral and multilateral contacts and either totally ignoring or flatly rejecting any claims of validity and truth on the part of secular ideologies and movements.

The same must be said of those Christians who interpret positively the accelerated process of secularization. In this century the term "secularization" has come to signify a social and cultural process by which nonreligious beliefs, practices, and institutions increasingly replace religious ones in all spheres of life. This process is greatly welcomed by many contemporary theologians. Christianity itself has greatly contributed, they argue, to the collapse of the pantheon of all sorts of Christian and ecclesiastical idols. Dialectical theology, the "demythologization" of the Gospel, and the theology of the death-of-God have been able to remove valueless layers from around the kernel of the Christian faith. Prof. van de Pol could not agree more with this. For a few decades now we have been living in a post-Constantinian period. After almost sixteen hundred years the church has finally thrown off its medieval and Victorian labels and trappings, becoming again a servant and pilgrim church in a pluralistic and interdependent society.

Again the terms "secularization" and "post-Constantinian Christianity" are quite ambiguous. Shifting with great eagerness their emphasis to the area of social ethics and politics, in order to show that their influence has not been caught in a process of shrinkage, the Christian churches quite clearly and successfully prolong the Constantinian period. Their urge to identify with the world, to compete with the world and to maintain their multiple institutions for their achievements in the world, is as strong as ever. The separation from the established phase of secularization, the opposition to a bourgeois cultural Christianity, or the retreat to a spiritual charismatic point of departure, oddly enough, as I already indicated before, all frequently lead to a reinforcement of conventional Christianity and a conventional Christian conduct. Even the best modern theology, forcefully stressing again that humanity living in time and space has, by God's grace, extraordinary possibilities of experiencing a radical transcendence, has not succeeded in inaugurating a new era of new collective Christian life expressing a greater desire to live less vis-à-vis and more really in the midst of this world.

I may add here in parentheses that even the defenders of secularism are on a wrong track. The term "secularism" has to be distinguished from the term "secularization." Secularism refers to the systematic rejection of all religion and religious considerations in the interpretation of the world and human existence. Secularism is the heart of an antireligious ideology. Outspoken critics of Christianity believe that the process of secularization is irreversible, irrevocably leading to the end of the Christian religion as well as all other religions. The traditions of a Christian culture and spirituality, they assert, will be abolished by a "humanity without God." This position, too, is untenable. Christianity, declared dead for decades in the Soviet Union and other communist states, has survived in contradiction to all ideological prognostics and political measures. The churches have once again been recognized by the state and have acquired an unexpected dynamic. The Christian religion and its complex ecclesiastical apparatus have by no means been eliminated. The phenomenon also of new religions coming into existence on all continents—Japan is a very good example—disproves the theory of the irreversibility of secularization.

Since hardly anything has weakened the solid base of institutional Christianity and challenged the power of the churches' structures, one may wonder whether or not the twentieth-century ecumenical movement has not to some extent changed and modified the thought and conduct of the world Christian community. This movement is after all known for its serious and prolonged efforts to bring the churches closer together, to update their international mission, to avoid much costly duplication and competition in work and service, and to face more honestly and humbly autonomous multireligious and secular society. The twentieth-century ecumenical movement has been inspired by great pioneers of vision and hope. Turning now to this movement, we shall see that even ecumenical Christianity still has immense difficulties in situating itself more maturely and gracefully in our "global village." In spite of all its inspiration to conceive of that village as one little macrocosm and to directly relate the rich to the poor, it has not assimilated itself to the Third World. Still worse, it has overrated the possibilities of becoming a part of and curing Calcutta's atrocious misery.

2

TWENTIETH-CENTURY
ECUMENICAL CHRISTIANITY

The World Council of Churches' Central Committee meeting at Rolle, Switzerland, in 1951, stated that the word "ecumenical" is "properly used to describe anything that relates to the whole task of the whole church to bring the Gospel to the whole world."[1] That task was already taken seriously at the International Missionary Conference in Edinburgh in 1910, when Anglican and Protestant missionaries expressed their conviction that divisions among Christians were a powerful obstacle to the spread of Christianity. A new evangelical concern brought about the formation, in 1921, of the International Missionary Council, comprising a large number of national missionary organizations. From 1939 its close association with the World Council of Churches, while that Council was in process of formation, continued until 1961 when the International Missionary Council was integrated in the World Council and became its Division of World Mission and Evangelism.

The ecumenical movement, as it developed during this century, flowed through two other streams of ecumenical endeavor. Bishop Charles Brent, an American Episcopalian who attended the Edinburgh Conference, launched a proposal for a conference on Faith and Order to which should be invited representatives of "all Christian communions throughout the world which confess the Lord Jesus Christ as God and Saviour." The first fully constituted World Conference on Faith and Order took place at Lausanne in 1927. Three other world conferences followed at Edinburgh (1937), Lund

(1952), and Montreal (1963). All Faith and Order meetings were not only concerned with exploring ways of organic church union but also with seeking together a common mind on various matters of Christian theology.

The third strand of ecumenism in Christendom had a service aspect and was of ethical significance. This strand came to be known as "Life and Work." In 1925 the Universal Christian Conference on Life and Work was convened at Stockholm in order to study the application of Christian principles to international relations and to social, industrial, and economic life. This movement went forward under the slogan "Service unites, doctrine divides." The report of the Oxford Life and Work Conference (1937) remains until today the most comprehensive ecumenical statement on problems of church and society covering the responsibility of Christians in many political, international, social, and economic realms. The Third World Conference on Church and Society, held in Geneva in 1966, witnessed the sharpest confrontation so far of the technological expertise of the western industrialized world with the revolutionary politics of the Third World, especially Latin America.

Since its founding at the Amsterdam Assembly in 1948, the World Council of Churches has grown into a large organization, increased its activities, and widened its international relations. Four other assemblies were held at Evanston (1954), New Delhi (1961), Uppsala (1968), and Nairobi (1975). The membership of the Council now consists of 293 churches from over 90 countries on six continents, including practically all confessions and denominations except the Roman Catholic church. The aims of the World Council are continuously carried out through its Assembly, its Central and Executive Committees, and through its staff organization in Geneva.

In 1971 the Council's headquarters in Geneva was given a new structure. Faith and Order, World Mission and Evangelism, and Church and Society, the three movements which led to the formation of the World Council of Churches, are now grouped together as three subunits of Programme Unit I. This unit carries the name "Faith and Witness." The title "Justice and Service" has been given to Programme Unit II, because it is increasingly recognized that Christian service to humanity cannot be separated from the church's struggle for justice. This unit is divided into four subunits, namely the Commission of the Churches' Participation in Development, the Programme to Combat Racism, the Commission of the Churches in International Affairs, and the Commission of Interchurch Aid, Refugee and World Service. The general functions of the unit as a whole are spelled out as follows:

To mobilize the contribution of Christians and their churches towards a world community based on freedom, peace and justice; to promote ecumenical reflections and actions on the Christian responsibility in development, racism, international affairs and other issues in contemporary world society; to help mobilize the whole people of God, irrespective of their organizational relationship to the World Council of Churches, in the fields of service, development, justice and peace.[2]

Programme Unit III includes various concerns and programs of education, women, youth, laity, and renewal action groups. It was therefore given the name "Education and Renewal."

Although the World Council of Churches has been a servant of the ecumenical movement and has done much during more than twenty-five years to promote concerns for unity, mission, and service throughout Christendom it should not be forgotten that the Council itself is not the ecumenical movement. There are other churches, in particular the Roman Catholic church, not belonging to the World Council, which are part of the ecumenical movement and strive for the unity of all Christians. The Vatican Secretariat for Promoting Christian Unity, established by Pope John XIII in 1960, has been active in its relationships with the World Council of Churches and individual churches. The term "Catholic ecumenism" is hardly used anymore. Ever since the close of the Second Vatican Council, the Roman Catholic church and the World Council of Churches have been in close cooperation, participating mutually in many conferences, and sponsoring a number of joint programs. Nevertheless, the question whether the Roman Catholic church will eventually join the fellowship of the World Council of Churches is still wide open.

Besides the international organization of the World Council of Churches there are numerous national and regional ecumenical bodies, many·of them associated or affiliated with the Council. The National Council of the Churches of Christ in the United States of

America, for instance, has continued since 1950 the work of the Federal Council of the Churches in America. It has various divisions and commissions on Church and Society, Overseas Ministries, Faith and Order, Regional and Local Ecumenism, Justice, Liberation, and Human Fulfillment. There is also a large Department on Church World Service, to which I referred earlier. The British Council of Churches, inaugurated in 1942, deals equally with a number of matters of national concern such as Ecumenical Affairs, and runs a Christian Aid Unit, which I also mentioned earlier. The Conference of Missionary Societies in Great Britain and Ireland, founded in 1912, works in association with the British Council of Churches. Among the several regional organizations I name only the Christian Conference of Asia, continuing the activities of the East Asia Christian Conference. From its headquarters in Singapore it is actively engaged in three programs: Message and Communication, Life and Action, Justice and Service.

Reference should be made also to the various international confessional organs of which the Lutheran World Federation is the largest organization. Located in the Ecumenical Center in Geneva, it runs a Department of Studies, a Department of Church Cooperation, and a Department of World Service, which are subdivided into several activities with a world scope. The twentieth-century ecumenical movement is further propelled by numerous newly emerging Christian communities and groups, all trying out spontaneous and new forms of worship, witness, and action in local and international settings. Despite the problems these groups and communities often pose to the institutional churches and their ecumenical organs, they are to be recognized as a creative challenge to historical ecumenical attitudes. Ecumenical Christianity, finally, embraces every man and woman trying to advance the dignity and quality of human community, hoping for the salvation of all humankind, and living their faith in nothing less than a global environment.

The Word "Ecumenical"

After this very short introduction to the twentieth-century ecumenical movement we are now in a better position to review more closely the etymology of the word "ecumenical." In the New Testament the Greek word *oikoumene* meant the "inhabited earth" in contrast to the uninhabited part of the world. In Greek "antiquity" and during the later period of Hellenism the concept was related to the realm of Greek culture, and this more in a historical than geographical sense. In the Roman Empire the word referred to the domain of the political commonwealth. Within the Roman Catholic church the term was applied for many centuries to those councils and creeds of the church that were universally accepted, as distinct from local synods and creeds. Only during this century has the word "ecumenical" been connected with the worldwide unity and mission of the church of Jesus Christ. Thus the ecumenical movement has become known as the movement toward the recovery of the unity of all believers in Christ, transcending differences of creed, ritual, and policy, as well as an interdenominational cooperation in missions.

Although a number of Christians have indicated that the ecumenical movement not only encompasses the unity and mission of all Christian churches but also originates in the unity of all people and the unity of all things in Jesus Christ, the serious question recurs as to whether the ecumenical movement is worldwide orientated and embraces all humankind without any reserve and discrimination. There is much evidence that the word "ecumenical," which early Christians borrowed from the Greek and Roman terminology, has not been newly interpreted and extended to the entire globe by contemporary ecumenical Christianity. The ecumenical space of antiquity was, after all, limited and did not comprise all human beings. A clear distinction was made between an inhabited world governed by divine order and blessed with cultural-political stability, and a surrounding barbarian world subject to meaninglessness and chaos. Since the Constantinian era, the concept of catholicity was applied only to the western *oikoumene;* where the mission of the church had not yet penetrated and been joyfully accepted, the mystery of the unity and concord of Christianity could not be comprehended.

The Greek term *oikoumene* is related to the Greek word *oikos*. This word not only refers to a house or a large building but is connected with the occupants, the family, and its descendants. The *oikeioi* are the fellow occupants, fully integrated into God's communion. The Jewish-Hellenistic philosopher Philo applied the word *oikos* to the church as the spiritual temple of God. This short analysis of the term *oikoumene* makes it clear that it is perfectly justified to ask whether the word contains today something other or more than notions of a civilized world, a spiritual realm, a worldwide mission, cultural expansion, a large family dwelling, and a universal Christian council. At least the history of the ecumenical movement suggests that Christianity has been too greatly preoccupied with putting its own "international house" in order to be in a position "to convert all others to its Lord Jesus Christ." After 1948 the words "heathen," "pagan," and "poor" were dropped and replaced by "secular," "multi-religious," and "underdeveloped." But the idea still persisted that the "non-Christian" parts of the word must be conformed to the orderly and peaceful Christian world. All international missionary gatherings since 1910 have served to strengthen the Christian consciousness of being called to deliver the world outside the *oikoumene* of false religion, irreligion, and unbelief. The missionary enthusiasm and zeal of all the carefully prepared world meetings led Christians everywhere to the conviction that God had called them to transform and to incorporate the marginal world into his meaningful and well-designed *oikoumene*.

There is no doubt that many alert and sensitive Christians today are aware of the dangerous state of human estrangement in which the institutionalized ecumenical movement has found itself. They earnestly wonder whether the imperative of dialogue among world religions, the encounter with contemporary ideologies, the growth of new secular nations, the tensions among races and cultures, and the search for political responsibility have led to a real change in the too self-assertive and too triumphant ecumenical attitude. They are not sure that the ecumenical dialogue has been widened by new servants who have drawn the attention of participants to major issues which were until then avoided or neglected. They tend to conclude that the church as a whole, in spite of its international orientation, is still marked by self-contemplation and self-approbation. Continuously nurtured by an overdiligence in its own affairs and an overconfidence in its very own cause, it still cannot generously, humbly, and without fear face the entire "non-Christian" world as it should. No wonder the ecumenical movement seems unable to affirm its true and peculiar Christian identity in the midst of the nations.

These arguments can be reinforced by testing the authenticity of the ecumenical movement against the Fourth World's predicament. The image of the *oikos* is invalid, for God's mission, in which Christians humbly participate, cannot mean bringing many thousands of persons who dwell in huts and urban shacks and on the streets safely into the ecumenical house. Also the idea of slowly incorporating the downtrodden and the impoverished into the more stable and civilized Christian world society has to be dropped entirely. Not only is the imagery around the words *oikoumene* and *oikos,* as used in ancient times, out-of-date, but twentieth-century ecumenical attitudes and methods have to be analyzed more critically. There is no longer a mission of the inhabited to the uninhabited world, a transfer of religious resources by the "haves" to the "have-nots." The deprived and the exploited will not be happier tomorrow if only they accept some of the advantages of an industrial and technological civilization. Both the rich and the poor are spiritually or materially deprived people. There is only one human race, sorely in need of forgiveness, reconciliation, and healing. The staggering difficulties of the East and South cannot be removed by western reasoning and massive aid. Christian missions share in the same fate of ineffectiveness. A well-formulated and well-presented Gospel alone will not enrich superstitious and unbelieving masses of people.

Intellectualism and activism among members of the white race are enemies of twentieth-century ecumenical Christianity. The word "ecumenical," we read, describes "anything that relates to the whole task of the whole church to bring the Gospel to the whole world." Today this definition must be severely challenged. It not only smacked of paternalism and condescension but also of elitism and rationalism. Only well-educated and articulate people, safely assembled in the *oikos,* were able to express themselves in such a neat formula. The World Council of Churches has been criticized for conducting its business meetings in a western parliamentary style. With its stress on representative democracy, the Anglo-Saxon parliamentary system is a procedure suited to bringing about an agreement on all matters where no unanimous decision can be reached. That criticism was one-sided and incomplete. The belief itself that secondary education and theological training are necessary to work out a sound ecumenical theology and strategy for Christian mission had far more disastrous effects. The whole notion of an established civilized world and exporting the treasures of that educated and experienced world was wrong. The "whole church" consists not only of intelligent and skillful Christians. The "whole world" comprises more than followers of Jesus Christ and other people, eventually to be converted and saved. The "whole task" of the church was improperly defined when pious and spirited activists had the only say. The Rolle definition of the word "ecumenical" lacked honesty and humility. It alluded too exclusively to the twofold idea that the church is principally divorced from the world and that it has sufficient strength to excel and to overcome that world.

One can argue that the earlier definition of the word "ecumenical" is now more than a quarter of a century old and no longer expresses the hopes and concerns of the present generation. The Nairobi Assembly reformulated the functions and purposes of the World Council of Churches, laid down in the Constitution and amended by the Uppsala Assembly. The Council's second, fourth, and fifth functions are now spelled out as follows:

to facilitate the common witness of the churches in each place and all places; to express the common concern of the churches in the service of human need, the breaking down of barriers between people, and the promotion of one human family in justice and peace; to foster the renewal of the churches in unity, worship, mission and service.[3]

Granted that the wording of the functions and aims has been improved, the idea that the church (as subject) ministers to the world (as object) recurs. There is little notion that the evangelization of the world—not surprisingly the sentence: "To support the churches in their world-wide missionary and evangelistic task" in the old constitution has been retained in the new constitution—the breaking down of barriers between people and the promotion of one human family in justice and peace are very delicate and intricate matters involving a subject-to-subject relationship. There is not sufficient awareness that other people are not to be taken into the one human family but belong already to that family and care in their way for that community. Only from the subject-object point of view does it make sense to emphasize that the strengthening and the rejuvenation of the churches is one of the foremost goals to be achieved. I will return to this point in a moment.

Even if the worldwide missionary enterprise is now seen in a somewhat more sober perspective and the rendering of a common witness is to be accomplished today in each place, ecumenical mission will come to a halt in Calcutta. There is no room for Christian intellectuals and activists in that city. The most pertinent and up-to-date ecumenical documents, translated into Bengali, Hindi, or Urdu, are inaccessible to vast crowds of Indian illiterates. Even if they could read, they would not have a clue as to what ecumenical literature is all about. Billy Graham will not succeed in organizing an evangelistic rally in Calcutta's Eden Gardens. The invited cannot decipher a page of the Bible and are far too hungry and tired to come forward to accept Jesus Christ as Lord and Savior. Indeed, only those who still claim to belong to the evangelical shock troops speak in ringing tones about their tremendous task and believe in the urgency of their verbal mission. But Christian activism and intellectualism crash head-on against Calcutta's wall of ignorance, passivism, and despair. Comforting words and seemingly unselfish actions will not breach a hole in that wall.

What Calcutta needs first of all is a most simple presence, a humble solidarity, and an all-out identification with its monstrous and hopeless human problems. Many churches, however, still continue to organize missionary consultations and conferences in order to formulate even better the contents of the Christian message and to "reach out" still further to confused and miserable corners of this earth. Little attention is paid to the fact that the continual spelling out of the relevance of the Gospel to the impoverished world and the uninterrupted redefining of the concept of ecumenical mission only obstruct the very human task of *listening* to those who have little to say and *being* with those who are hardly capable of acting.

For that very reason one is not surprised that mission and dialogue—to speak in the current intellectual ecumenical language—are still much opposed notions in the ecumenical movement. Leading churchmen are still worried that dialogue will weaken mission and lead to syncretism. Dialogue suggests that Christianity is only one religion among many. This cannot be accepted, as Christians will be in danger of losing their identity. Many other Christians argue that dialogue can take place only if it leads to "making strangers into fellow-citizens in the household of God." How embarrassing is all this rationalization of the church's mission. How poor and sterile are the monologues on the danger and limits of dialogue. They do not make Christians credible ambassadors of reconciliation. Not mission but dialogue is the one and only hope for the failing hearts of Calcutta's multitudes. I will discuss more fully the obstacles, the requirement, and the promise of dialogue in the next two chapters.

A Truly Universal Council

Just as ecumenical missions hardly reach the countless wretched of this world, so too ecumenical matters of Faith and Order must be seriously questioned in the context of disintegrating societies. We have seen that for many centuries the term "ecumenical" has been related to a general or universal council of the church. The usage of the word in this sense has been revived during the past few years. The Fourth Assembly at Uppsala (1968) indicated that:

the World Council of Churches may be regarded as a transitional opportunity for eventually actualizing a truly universal, ecumenical, conciliar form of common life and witness.

The same Assembly also suggested that the member churches of the Council:

should work for the time when a genuinely universal council may once more speak for all Christians, and lead the way into the future.[4]

It was necessary to express serious doubts whether the whole inhabited earth finds an appropriate place within the ecumenical movement having as its primary aim to bring an all-embracing World Council of Churches into existence. Despite the concern that further discussion of the theme of a "truly universal council" is only possible in connection with an "expression of deep care for the whole of humanity," and despite the affirmation that the interpretation of this theme depends on the right understanding of "God's design for the whole world," revealed in Jesus Christ, the search for and the eventual creation of a universal council had still the odor of a sectarian enterprise. Not a more tolerable life for many parts of the world but a more perfect life of the universal church was still foremost at stake.

The present ecumenical "councils" were evidently not yet characterized by true conciliarity, which was an essential mark of the great councils of the early church. Precisely that conciliarity had to be updated and amplified. All conciliar groups—local, national, and regional councils—international confessional organizations, and the World Council of Churches were urged to examine their life and action in the light of true conciliarity. Close cooperation among the churches, among the World Council of Churches, the Vatican Secretariat for Promoting Christian Unity, and many other Christian groups outside the World Council could lead to the permanent establishment of a genuinely universal council. Recently the idea and aim of eventually creating such a truly universal council have fallen into the background. The one church is now increasingly more

envisioned as a conciliar fellowship of local churches which are themselves truly united. In this conciliar fellowship, each local church possesses, in communion with the others, the fullness of catholicity, witnesses to the same apostolic faith and, therefore, recognizes the others as belonging to the same Church of Christ and guided by the same spirit.[5]

The church in each place and in all places gathers God's people around the personal presence of Christ in the ministry of word and sacrament acknowledged and accepted by all.

Whether in a world or local perspective the image of the ecumenical family house is still valid. The mansions must be enlarged and renovated to bring still more Christians into spacious, safe, and permanent dwellings. All people in affluent societies live in solidly constructed houses and well-equipped apartments. Buildings are signs of human culture and ingenious technology. Their roofs and walls protect men and women against the whims of nature. Houses provide for a sense of belonging, stability, and protection. The Christian churches in Europe spent billions of dollars after 1945 to rebuild cathedrals, chapels, and meetinghouses and to indulge in costly church architectural phantasies. Many ecumenical gatherings take place in impressive auditoriums. The latest World Council of Churches Assembly was held in a huge, ultramodern, highly functional, and very fascinating conference center in Nairobi, Kenya. One wonders what the new building for the truly universal council of churches will look like and where it will be erected.

In the poverty-stricken cities and the immense rural areas of the Third and Fourth Worlds the imagery of solid dwellings, ecumenical *oikoi,* is for two thirds of the world's population void of meaning. The solemn first assembly of the genuinely universal council of churches will not arouse their enthusiasm and will not "show them the way forward into the future." Solid and impressive local church build-ings do not offer them real human protection and security. The word "ghetto" originally referred to a quarter of a city in which Jews were required to live. For 2 billion people Christian churches and their edifices are not much more than well-separated and secure ghettos in the midst of the nations struggling for survival. And the *oikoumene* under the roof of a truly universal council is in their eyes not more than an international ghetto in a world of turmoil and want.

Yet the Basis of the World Council of Churches, formulated in 1948 and revised in 1961, still stands. This Basis reads:

The World Council of Churches is a fellowship of churches which confess the Lord Jesus Christ as God and Saviour according to the Scriptures and therefore seek to fulfil together their common calling to the glory of the one God, Father, Son and Holy Spirit.[6]

The first part of the Basis deals clearly with the *visible* existence of the churches, their international gatherings, and their obligation to formulate jointly their witness. The *oikoumene,* therefore, depends in the first place on the institutional structures of the churches and their conciliar testimony, which is inspired by the faith that God reconciles humanity in Jesus Christ. It cannot be granted that all human beings are fundamentally and identically included in God's plan of salvation, regardless of the range and the result of conciliar witness. The faith and not the fact that God deals with all men and women needs to be strengthened by the right ecclesiology and a well-defined theology of mission. God's dealing with humanity can become transparent only in the ecumenical movement which is on its way to become the one and true church of Jesus Christ. Thus the Basis of the Word Council of Churches has in the first instance a delimitative and exclusive function. Like the original word *oikoumene,* it keeps the "inhabited world of faith" apart from the "uninhabited world without faith."

All these contemporary theological and ecclesiological exercises in an ecumenical framework are of no help to the world's abandoned peoples. They do not ask to be admitted to God's magnificent *oikoi.* They have no desire to read and to understand world Christian literature. They do not wish to be elected as delegates to the truly universal council of churches. All they need is immediate help, not only food, clothing, and shelter but also human presence and assistance which makes God's unconditional love for all creatures transparent. It is not true that the more the churches are united, the more the world will believe. On the contrary, the more the churches organize themselves in large international associations, the more they speak of the mystery of the *one* Body of Christ, and the more they desire to move massively into areas of acute need and distress, keeping the will and the integrity of the people to "develop themselves" in mind, the more the millions of deprived and exploited will be crushed. In Calcutta's society the term "God's people" must include far more than a world company of believers in concord and unity. The Body of Christ cannot be limited to those who earnestly search for a supreme manifestation of the church's conciliarity and catholicity. Calcutta "affirms" that God's love wholly surpasses the churches' charitable and humanitarian actions in many regions and localities of this world. But precisely this fact is not implicitly acknowledged in ecumenical circles. Christians and their churches are on the contrary so absorbed in drawing up multiple programs of relief, aid, and assistance that little or no room is left to God's uncontrollable action and radical intervention.

Interchurch Aid and Social Programs

On that ground the second part of the World Council of Churches' Basis: ". . . and therefore seek to fulfil together their common calling . . ." can indeed be interpreted as a continuous attempt to review the joint endeavors of the Christian churches. It is not just a coincidence that in the formulation of the aims and functions of the council's Programme Unit II, "Justice and Service," and its subunits, the words "Christians" and "churches" are precisely the ones which are always emphasized. "The contribution of *Christians* and their *churches* towards a world community based on freedom, peace and justice" is to be mobilized. "Concern in the *churches* for the protection and implementation of human rights" should be activated. "*Christian* participation in the just resolution of international conflicts" must be stimulated and assisted. *"The whole people of God"* should be enlisted in "the fields of service, development, justice and peace" (italics mine).

Of course, the World Council of Churches and all other international, regional, and national organizations as instruments and service agencies of the churches, have no other choice than to contribute to programs of development for underdeveloped countries, to facilitate the transfer of human and material resources for social welfare, to fight a worldwide racism, to plead for the dignity of humanity, to promote the spirit of reconciliation and human solidarity in political affairs, to render medical services to the sick, and to face many acute emergencies. As humanity's injustice to humanity and the injustice of nations to nations do not decrease, collective charitable action must be initiated and carried out. Likewise, systematic attempts must be made to facilitate the sharing of material supplies and human abilities in a more equal and just way.

Still, this refined and sensible ecumenical language inspires suspicion and fear if one looks with Calcutta's anguished and starving population to the well-structured Christian organizations specializing in aid, relief, and rescue. One is not sure at all whether the *oikoumene,* dealing with human and humanitarian problems, really exists for the sake of the desperate world or whether the desperate world exists only for the sake of the universal church. Many international interchurch aid conferences at least create the impression that Christians are experts in relieving others from the burdens of evil, want, and distress. The temptation persists to transform the very real needs of the troubled world into the institutional affairs of numerous ecclesiastical organizations. The defeated world itself thus serves as an external environment for the ecumenical bodies and their constituencies' charitable and social activities. The many national and international agencies of the Roman Catholic church should, of course, be included here. All these activities are, in fact, not direct but only indirect responses to and aligned to the world "outside."

The conclusion must be drawn that there is only one normative pattern of civilized and humanitarian assistance to the underdeveloped nations, namely, that of the experienced Christian church. The ecumenical movement is in the end not identified with the compassion, justice, and reconciliation of the Lord Jesus Christ, but with the obligations of church organizations equipped to render a manifold service. It is indeed very difficult to look behind and beyond ecumenical action groups that are deliberately composed of the widest possible Christian representation of different regions, traditions, and intellectual and spiritual points of view. Fascinated by the multicultural and multiconfessional composition of such gatherings, one becomes convinced that the ecumenical movement equals the churches' search for unity and their contributions to justice, equality, and peace in whatever difficult situation.

So far my critique of ecumenical Christianity has been as harsh and severe as of Christianity in general. But if one has visited Calcutta and still frequently remembers the thousands of filthy, sick, and wretched people, one has no other choice than to look *in the midst of them* and *with them* toward the Christian churches around the world. Ecumenical reflections, church programs, and energetic Christian actions appear then in a quite different light. To the degree that these reflections, programs, and actions originate within and are conditioned by Christian constituencies, to that extent they fail to really penetrate into the human situation of those whose survival, health, dignity, and ultimate salvation are at stake. Standing outside the structures and the frontiers of the churches, one cannot help notice that the churches' own existence and their own particular future still seem to be the primary issues, regardless of whether matters of precious unity, exceptional mission, or distinct service are taken up. All too often the style and language of ecumenical literature is ambiguous and even misleading since it supposes that millions of other people can think in similar ecumenical categories and accept equal responsibilities in facing their own political and socioeconomic situation.

For several years now it has been a standard ecumenical practice in Christian service agencies to deal with "counterparts," that is, groups of indigenous people who themselves draw up projects for development and make their own decisions about their nations' potentials and priorities. For many years churches and individual Christians have given serious attention to the application and protection of human rights in all countries of the world. In the field of ecumenical education it is more and more stressed that the central educational concern is with whatever sharpens a people's awareness of the dilemmas and possibilities in its culture, history, environment, and political power. Critical consciousness must become a worldwide priority. Christian theologians and laypersons, preoccupied with church and society matters, more and more urge oppressed peoples to engage themselves in direct political struggles and to do away with the basic causes of injustice. Referring to the Jewish and Christian idea of human domination over nature, and quoting Genesis and Saint Paul, poor nations are encouraged to apply industrial and technological "know-how" to their countries' underdeveloped economies. In the area of missions it is continuously assured that the Bible contains all the truth people need to know and that obedience to God's Word prevents them from becoming indifferent to others' needs and from making grave social mistakes.

The list of ecumenical counsels and encouragements can be further extended. But at the same time this whole list of Christian recommendations is to be exposed to a great number of questions. How many "counterparts" exist and qualify for a very demanding and complicated task? For how many millions is the fundamental right to human dignity no more than a phrase on a piece of paper, unrelated to the agony of their undernourished body and tortured mind? How many people have developed a "critical consciousness"? How do people suffering injustice become aware of the causes of their situation? As other religions stress the harmony of humanity and nature and increasingly discover that there is nothing in Christianity that points to such a harmony, how are these world religions to recommend technological advance to their faithful? How can the Bible be interpreted not literally but translated into very different religious and cultural contexts? How can "indigenous theologies" escape the accusation of deviationism and heresy?

All these questions are crucial but they are still of a secondary nature. The profound question behind all these questions is whether the churches and their ecumenical organs are not disavowing the very Gospel itself by commending the message of liberation and reconciliation from their own historical, intellectual, and cultural perspectives. The Sermon on the Mount addresses the poor in spirit, the sorrowful, the mourners, the merciful, the pure in heart, and the peacemakers. It is they who inherit the kingdom of heaven; it is they who receive mercy and find consolation; it is they who will see God and will be called his children. This message does not come from a civilized world and its content is not formulated by Christian activists. It does not even lend itself to missionary and educational purposes. The sermon defies all pious attempts to classify the pure in heart, to comfort the sorrowful and mourning, to educate the poor in spirit, and to assist the peacemakers. It turns the whole idea of an "inhabited" and an "uninhabited world" upside-down. It challenges the meaning of the word "ecumenical" if this term does not denote more than a mission of the "saved" to those "to be saved." According to Matthew 5 the "to be saved" are saved and have a mission to those who seem to be saved. One wonders whether the concept *oikoumene* should not be dropped altogether if it still alludes to an eventual widening of the international realm of Christian influence and to a series of spiritual and moral advancements in the midst of a bewildering and contradictory "non-Christian" world.

Yet the word carries in itself the notion of the entire world and the entire human race. The *oikoumene* anticipates nothing less than the one unity of all men, women, and children before God. Can Christians truly rejoice in this anticipation and leave without worry ample room for the most passive, unobtrusive, unconventional, ineffective, and inarticulate human beings? Can they freely admit that even articulate and active people with very different beliefs, opinions, and expectations are not excluded from God's *oikoumene*? Can Christians be motivated to enter with all these groups of human beings into living relationships and to share with them very different ultimate convictions and hopes?

The reinterpretation of "ecumenical" in this sense can take place only if several heavy obstacles are removed from the traditional ecumenical road. Among these obstacles are Christianity's claim to absolute validity, the problem of syncretism, and the reluctance to accept fully the present pluralistic world situation. They continue to block the official church position and the Christian mind to such an extent that the challenge to a universal openness is still today not widely accepted and honestly faced. We will deal with these obstructions on the ecumenical highway in a moment. As the church does not relinquish its claim to be the unique bearer of the absolute truth, the very dialogue between people of living faiths and contemporary ideologies hardly progresses and causes much dissension and confusion. Although some significant ecumenical attempts have been made to develop a common vision concerning the dialogue with people of other faiths, they have so far not aroused wide enthusiasm. Fundamental differences of opinion as to this problem have remained within the World Council of Churches and the churches themselves. Many church leaders are alarmed and distrustful of groups of "too progressive" Christians pushing the dialogue issue too far within the Christian community.

But exactly these tensions and conflicts can revive the ecumenical movement and steer it into a new and more promising direction. No single world religion, including Christianity, can claim to have a definitive answer to the question of why humanity is divided into many religious and ideological groups. The church as much as any other religious community is not by its nature in a better position to explain why the emerging world society is composed of various faiths and convictions. Nobody can say with any certainty today what the future of world religions will be. Only one thing is very sure. If Buddhists, Christians, Hindus, Jews, Muslims, and still other people of different faiths do not start, and continue, to reflect and to live together, all the Calcuttas will have to be written off as insolvable religious and ideological problems. The afflicted and debased peoples are the test for the authenticity and relevance of all world religions, including the world Christian religion. The dialogue in the midst of, and for the sake of, these peoples is not an optional enterprise, a friendly comparing of religious notes, and a leisurely spelling out of some common religious denominators, but a matter of life and death of the finest and deepest religious convictions, even of the most precious Christian doctrinal convictions. To this dialogue I will turn after a short examination of the obstacles to universal dialogue produced within Christianity itself.

3

OBSTACLES TO THE
INTER-RELIGIOUS DIALOGUE

A spiritual encounter and intellectual dialogue between Christianity and other world religions has begun only during the second part of the twentieth-century, in consequence of radical changes in the religious, socio-political, and economic situation of the world. For almost two millennia Christianity has adopted a negative attitude to the truth and values of "non-Christian" religions. All adherents of superstitious beliefs were categorically excluded from eternal salvation. Like Judaism, the early church viewed the pagan gods as humanly fabricated idols, incomparable with the one and true living God, Creator of the world, and Redeemer of humanity. Faith in Jesus Christ meant deliverance from all primitive heathen religion, from veneration of stone or bronze images of deities made by human beings, and a fierce struggle against the enslaving evil and demonic forces. When Islam was founded in the seventh century as a new higher religion, Christianity fought it bitterly as a Christian heresy. The apocalyptic interpretation of Islam as the religion of the "false prophet" led to the archetypal struggle of the Christian church of the Middle Ages against foreign religions, namely, to the crusade.

Although the fifteenth-century German theologian Nicolas of Cusa called for the establishment of peace among world religions and the philosophy of the Enlightenment demanded tolerance between followers of different religious teachings, the missions conducted in the eighteenth and nineteenth centuries entirely ignored this knowledge or consciously rejected it. The Roman Catholic church since Francis Xavier and the Protestant missionary societies since the rise of Pietism and Methodism were concerned only with the conversion of pagan souls, which were regarded as needing to be rescued into the eternal church. There was not the slightest awareness that Christianity, as a product of culture, as a world religion, could in many ways obstruct the arrival of God's kingdom rather than promote it. Only in this century did the church slowly enter into direct contact with all living "non-Christian" religions; and only after World War II, when many former mission churches were transformed into independent churches in the newly autonomous Asian and African states, did the concept of inter-religious dialogue find more open minds.

The same development occurred in the twentieth-century ecumenical movement. The major international missionary conferences hardly spoke of contact and exchanges with representatives of other religions but repeatedly emphasized the missionary obligation of the churches by pointing to the urgent task of evangelism. The International Missionary Council meeting in Jerusalem in 1928 made the Christian message its first consideration, especially in relation to modern secularism. At Tambaram, Madras, in 1938, the same Council engaged in a study of the Christian message in a non-Christian world. At the international gathering in Whitby, Ontario, in 1947, the Council set itself to discover the relevance of the Gospel to a world recovering from the war. At the next meeting in Willingen, Germany, in 1952, delegates of older and younger churches stated their belief in church unity as an essential condition for effective witness and advance. Only at the last Council meeting in Ghana, in 1958, did the word "communication" come to the forefront. A sympathetic listening to others was recommended; evangelism should take the form of communication, an interhuman conversation. Missionary societies and "younger churches" were encouraged to help formulate effective ways of presenting the Christian faith to the secular intelligentsia as well as to the devoted adherents of other religions.

The notions of the passing on of the message in the form of dialogue and a new way of approaching "non-Christians" came even more into force at the World Council's Third Assembly in New Delhi. The impact of Asian delegates, who were keen to interpret and to evaluate the world religions in a positive context, was felt.

Already at the First Assembly of the East Asia Christian Conference in 1958 a study called "The Word of God and the Living Faiths of Men" took shape and further suggestions were made to pay more attention to the interaction between religious beliefs and social changes.

The Second Assembly of the same Conference at Bangkok in 1964 urged Christians to enter into true conversations with people of other beliefs, whether religious or not. The World Council of Churches was in regular contact with more than fifteen study centers for dialogue and for the study of religion and society, most of them located in Asia and all of them having sufficient freedom to perform their pioneering task.

Still today these study centers help strengthen the life and witness of the churches by providing a place with an atmosphere conducive to research and worship, consultations and conferences, designed to help theological students and laymembers of the Christian community find a deeper understanding of the Christian faith in relation to the religious and social environment of their respective countries and regions. Many of them issue a journal or a bulletin and sponsor various studies in book or pamphlet form. In particular, the Christian Literature Society in Madras has published an enormous quantity of monographs dealing with subjects of an inter-religious nature. Unfortunately most of this outstanding and challenging literature of the last twenty years is little known in the West.

It was only at the World Council's Fourth Assembly at Uppsala that the Christian attitude to adherents of other religions was no longer confined to the particular sphere of "mission." Dialogue became now an important concern in itself within the ecumenical movement and was recognized as a lasting obligation in a world of various faiths, cultures, and ideologies. Already a World Council of Consultation on "Christian Dialogue with Men of Other Faiths" at Kandy, Sri Lanka, in 1967, in which Roman Catholics, Orthodox, and Protestants participated, had emphasized that fresh thinking was needed on questions relating to the place of other religious traditions in the economy of God's purpose for humankind. It further added that true illumination would only come through the actual experience of far more *living* in dialogue. Two major ecumenical and multilateral consultations have taken place so far. One was held in

Ajaltoun, Lebanon, in 1970, in which Buddhists, Christians, Hindus, and Muslims took part. The emphasis of the conversations was primarily on the experience of dialogue itself rather than on academic discussion about its nature and purpose. A second multilateral dialogue in Colombo, Sri Lanka, in 1974, brought together people of five different faiths, this time including Jews as well. One of the crucial questions raised at this gathering was whether there is a way that does justice to the commitment of a particular faith and at the same time recognizes the dimensions of universality.

These two multilateral and several bilateral dialogues were initiated and sponsored by the World Council of Churches' Secretariat on Dialogue with People of Living Faiths and Ideologies, created in 1969. Its mandate spelled out by the Council's Central Committee at Addis Ababa in 1971 stated that dialogue offers "the promise of discovering new dimensions of understanding our faith," opportunities for "new relationships between Christians and men of other faiths," and possibilities where our "Christian faith can be tested and strengthened." Dialogue also envisages cooperation with people of other faiths and ideologies on specific issues which "will involve not only study but also common action." The basis of the dialogue, the mandate asserted, is our faith in Jesus Christ, "who makes us free and draws us out of isolation into genuine dialogue into which we enter with faith in the promise of Jesus Christ that the Holy Spirit will lead us into all truth."[1]

Before discussing some of the insights and experiences of recent encounters among representatives of world religions, it is necessary to delineate the many reservations and oppositions to the inter-religious dialogue in the international Christian camp. As I indicated at the end of Chapter 2, two old anxieties have continued to overshadow the last ten years of reflection and commitment to ecumenical dialogue: the relativization of Christianity and the danger of syncretism. Both anxieties have haunted the Christian mind for a few centuries. Even today only a minority of Christians is able to admit that the whole discussion on the uniqueness of the Christian religion as the "crown" of all religions will remain sterile because it is conducted within the walls of the church itself and communicated afterwards to the world in an apologetic and aggressive manner. Too many Christians ignore that as long as the church is not caught up in a long and profound dialogue with the religious and secular world, it cannot but focus primarily on itself and prove that the truth can be only on its side. Also the argument of syncretism turns in a vicious circle, assuming something that still has to be defined and proved. The Gospel, therefore, has little chance of delivering Christians from a narrow-minded absolutism and intolerance toward other beliefs as long as they discuss the errors and pitfalls of other religions within their well-structured and "watertight" communities. The World Council's "Addis Ababa mandate" rightly spoke of the faith in Christ which makes free and draws out of petty isolation. Indeed, only freedom in the Lord, which is ever newly experienced in actually living together with people of other faiths and ideological convictions, can liberate Christians both from an undue intolerance and from the danger of becoming overtolerant and uncritical relativists. I will now briefly examine the self-defensive and militant Christian attitudes toward all other religions. These attitudes largely still prevail today.

The End of One Absolute Religion

In the late eighteenth century and during the ninteenth century, Christian missions made a totalitarian claim to the absolute truth, correctness, and value of the Christian religion, depreciating all other religions to a combination of superstition, idolatry, and incredulity. Slightly more politely, some argued that, unfortunately, in pagan religions the little truth is so grossly mixed up with error that the truth becomes insignificant. Conversion to Christianity can take place only after heathendom has been thoroughly cleansed from its fears, illusions, and erroneous beliefs. Early in this century liberal German theologians like Adolf von Harnack, Ernst Troeltsch, and Reinhold Seeberg, following in the footsteps of Hegel, designed a pyramid of religions and spoke of Christianity as the culminating and converging point of the religious development of humankind. Although certain values and truths of other religions were more deeply appreciated, there was no doubt that only the Christian religion qualifies to occupy the seat of honor and glory.

In the thirties and forties dialectical theology made a final grand attempt to draw a sharp dividing line between Christianity and the non-Christian religions. The Swiss theologian Karl Barth and his school developed a new negative concept of religion. According to Barth, religion is nothing but the attempt of a godless and wicked humanity to reach for God. In all their religious acts, men and women worship idols and elevate themselves to an imaginary level of adoration. Christianity is not a religion because it does not show the way to God, but reveals God's coming to humanity in Jesus Christ. The unique New Testament revelation is radically contrasted with all historical religions. While the Gospel is "emphatically theocentric," religions are "emphatically anthropocentric," Barth and his followers argued. Consequently, a comparative study of world religions—including Christianity understood as a religion—is of little or no value. A Christian knows beforehand that all religion is exclusively based on human inspiration and leads finally nowhere and thus to perdition.

One has to keep in mind that Karl Barth fashioned his theology in strong opposition to national socialism, a primitive but contagious cryptoreligious ideology. The exclusiveness of the revealed character of the Christian faith had to be stressed in order to make cooperation with both Nazism and the official church, which endorsed a curious brand of German Christianity and Rosenberg racism, quite impossible. On the other hand, Karl Barth, as a typical European theologian, had no first-hand knowledge of non-European cultures and knew the world religions only from academic textbooks written by Christian scholars. He had neither desire nor need to meet adherents to other faiths. One of his followers, the Dutch Islamic scholar Hendrik Kraemer, wrote a book entitled *The Christian Message in a Non-Christian World,* which evoked animated discussions during and after the International Missionary Council's conference at Tambaram, Madras, in 1938. Although Kraemer developed his thoughts in a less massive and negative theological language than Barth, many theologians, particularly in Asia, protested against this work, which attempted in its own way to expound the absolute character of Christianity and the total discontinuity between the Gospel and all religions that search desperately but in vain for a compassionate God.

The authoritarian Barth-Kraemer approach to religions is no longer acceptable today. Other neo-orthodox schools of theology also failed to do justice to the wisdom of sacred scriptures, the unflinching loyalty to the truth, the profound mystical experiences, and the outstanding sober life of many non-western faithful. The defense of one single revealed religion against all other humanly fabricated religions comes close to a dangerous solipsism. There is much evidence that zealous Christian theologians decided in advance to close their eyes and ears to whatever reality there might be in the insight, spirituality, and commitment of world religions. A comparative study of religions did not amount to more than using religious treasures of Buddhism, Hinduism, and Islam for a clever advocacy of the biblical truth. One simply was unable to see that a narrow and uncharitable doctrine of salvation is in contradiction with the symbol of the cross, the visible sign of world reconciliation, and that only a poor and thin Gospel can prosper on the heap of religious ruins. No wonder that Asian people were quite unable to discover the heart of the liberating Christian message, namely, the very lowliness and utter mercy of the Son of God.

Neo-orthodoxy, it is true, rightly opposed earlier liberal attempts to bring all religions under one roof. The argument that all religions are basically the same except for their mythology and ritual, and that each in its way leads to the same God, does not stand the test. It cannot be taken for granted that the many different religious experiences all point to the true nature and being of the one and only God. Also to elaborate a value scale of world religions and to classify Christianity at the top of that scale is to do injustice both to Christianity and to other religions. But modern western theology, on the other hand, became very undialectical when, instead of offering an inclusive God it offered an exclusive God and exchanged an inclusive world Christ for an exclusive western Christ. By trying to immunize the western church against both uncritical theological liberalism and secular idolatry, it left the world outside the Atlantic community to its own fate. Neo-orthodoxy could flourish only as long as it was isolated from and unchallenged by the other religions.

In the latter part of this book we shall see that the western defense of the revealed and absolute truth in Jesus Christ is not only presumptuous but preposterous in the setting of "non-Christian" societies. It is even more disastrous to exploit the truth of the cross for a fierce struggle against the deceptions and falsifications of

human religion in the Fourth World. The agony and impotence of
Jesus Christ on the cross, which will speak for themselves to those
who agonize and are impotent, are rendered offensive and incredible through futile theological attempts to prove their divine design
and value. Walter Hollenweger once pointedly said that "a missionary risks his own understanding of the Gospel by communicating it."[2]
That process of communication in Calcutta has indeed nothing to do
with introducing one's own discernment of the exclusive traits of the
only saving God and arguing about his effective ways of dealing with
humanity, in particular with its most destitute and pitiful parts. It is
only through stammering utterances and a not very articulate communication that both we Christians and our "superstitious" fellow
human beings discover and rediscover the miracle of God's mercy
upon his entire creation. The agony and impotence of the cross
sustain both the poor and needy deliverer of a message and the poor
and needy receiver of that message. They truly liberate Christian
preachers from their presumption to be able to explain the healing
power of the cross as much as the listeners from their presumption to
be able to reject that healing power on the ground that the message
smacks of typical western apologetics.

The Sham Fight Against Syncretism

As there have always been Christians, both theologians and laity,
who have believed they were serving God by setting certain precise
limits to the Gospel, so too there have been many others who have
untiringly warned against a blending of Christianity with other religions. I refer here to the old problem of *syncretism*. The word has
been given various meanings and it is difficult to find an adequate
definition. If one speaks of syncretism in the sense of a particular
religion incorporating other religious ideas, customs, and rites in its
own theological system and practice, all world religions must be
called syncretistic. Any religion communicating to its environment
must use expressions and concepts of people living in their particular
milieu. Syncretism in this case can assume the function of "indigenization." The term should rather be reserved for various attempts
indiscriminately to patch together incompatible beliefs with the
object of creating a viable world religion for all humanity. Real

syncretism presupposes that there is no unique revelation in history and that it is necessary to combine and to harmonize different religious concepts and experiences in order to arrive at a fully universal religion. A distinction should also be made between syncretism and eclecticism, which denotes the choice of particular elements from different religious and philosophical systems and their combination into a new but frequently not very original system. Some Indian religious pioneers have tried unsuccessfully to introduce elements of Christian monotheism into Hinduism. Also the Baha'i religion is largely based on eclectic principles.

During the last two decades the whole question of syncretism once again became acute in 1963 when W. A. Visser't Hooft, the first General Secretary of the World Council of Churches, devoted a book entitled *No Other Name* to this delicate problem. The subtitle of the book was: *"The Choice Between Syncretism and Christian Universalism."* The author freely admits that the church has frequently promoted a kind of universalism which seems to be "concerned only with the Christian part of humanity." "No one can deny," he writes:

that Western Christianity has very often given the impression that it looked down on other religions and considered itself as the proud possessor of the truth. It is therefore understandable that those who know little of the foundations of Christianity consider Christians as arrogant and narrow-minded.[3]

But after this has been granted, he moves on to the "business" of the ecumenical movement. He agrees with Hendrik Kraemer that:

the Christian church . . . should first and foremost set her own house in order, because the greatest service she can render to the world is being resolutely the Church of Jesus Christ.[4]

Here we revert completely to the neo-orthodox attempt to define in advance the absolute character of God's revelation in Jesus Christ and the divine nature of his church. Only after the "ABC" of Christian theology has been spelled out can the dialogue of the religions take place. That dialogue is accepted somewhat reluctantly. "The churches will be called upon more and more frequently to co-operate with men of other faiths and no faith in matters of public life," Visser't Hooft states. And he adds immediately:

We will have to accept that new duty; . . . but we must make it perfectly plain that our willingness to co-operate does not in any way imply a willingness to compromise on the basic issues of the faith.[5]

Dialogue is a duty, not a challenge and a privilege. The conversations have to deal mainly with common tasks in the "pluriform national societies"; essential issues of faith can eventually be compared only with extreme care and great difficulty. When beginning a dialogue Christians had better inform their partners immediately that they will not yield an inch in their precious convictions. Such a "dialogue," of course, effectively exorcizes the ghost of syncretism. But if the dialogue partners are told by the Christian participants that they have only "the choice between syncretism and Christian universalism," the conversations will not be very helpful and inspiring. No true dialogue in fact is taking place.

Syncretism, indeed, remains a threat to all world religions. But Christian theologians have a special facility for blowing syncretism up to the proportions of a dangerous monster. If such a religious monster really exists, then, of course, Christians must beware of relativizing their faith by conversing with people of "uncertain and vague" opinions. In a truly syncretistic atmosphere the Christian church has no other choice than to put a strong emphasis on its own identity and integrity. It is, however, a false assumption in Christianity that the church is surrounded by syncretistic forces and even invited to participate in the search for a synthesis or confluence of the existing religions. Several recent multilateral religious dialogues have proved that humanity is not slowly on its way to fabricate a synthetic universal religion, a normative world faith for members of the world community. Such a combined faith is not only a poor alternative to religious conflict and an impoverishment of humanity but it will be strongly resisted by any major religion defending its own spiritual integrity. In the present dialogue Islam continues to uphold a very strict and consistent monotheism which guarantees the unity of the sacred and profane world. Hinduism, on the other hand, wishes to permeate the world, including the animal and vegetable world, with the divine spirit, which it cannot discover in the prophetic religions. Buddhism remains a real challenge to Christianity as it does not carry the stigma of an absolute religious claim and opposes an authoritarian approach to ethics and society with a total autonomy of the individual. Judaism does not show any inclination to share its messianic hope with Christianity and Islam.

The reason western missionary experts and theologians have talked so much about the all-pervasive dangers of syncretism is that they have far too often cut themselves off from living relationships with particular communities and cultures. Dialoguing about the pitfalls of dialogue in Christian circles, instead of fully and sincerely meeting adherents of other faiths in their very real environment and sharing their urgent concerns, does very quickly lead to a rather piteous devising of defense mechanisms and a mutual encouragement in the same Christian circles to convert others, who for some inexplicable reason resist the convincing power of the Gospel. Even if the former General Secretary of the World Council asserts that "the fact that Christians believe that they know the source of divine truth does not mean that they have nothing to learn from men of other faiths,"[6] it still remains difficult to interpret such apodictic words. There are also several seemingly polite and encouraging single sentences in official ecumenical statements indicating that dialogue is central for Christians living in a pluralistic society, but these isolated sentences have very little content and no real impact on the internal ecumenical debate. Unless Christians dare to speak of an *oikoumene* beyond the Christian churches, present and future ecumenical Christianity will still be excessively preoccupied with escaping the hazards of relativism and the risks of syncretism. A genuine encounter with adherents of other living faiths or contemporary ideological convictions can and will take place only if the church grasps afresh that only the Gospel itself liberates us both from a narrow-minded absolutism and an undue tolerance toward other beliefs or secular persuasions.

Other Inept and Unprofitable Arguments

Besides the argument of the discontinuity and the incompatibility of the Christian religion with all other religions and the rejection of

classic syncretism, which would mingle, reconcile, and unite con-
flicting beliefs into a hybrid world religion, other strong objections
to ongoing ecumenical reflection and its implications for inter-
religious dialogue are voiced by church groups, mission boards,
councils of churches, and their respective leaders. Quite recently the
word "neosyncretism" has been coined. Neosyncretism, according
to the users of this term, has two aspects. It blots out the demarcation
line between the church and the world and exchanges the kingdom
of God for a humanistically orientated world community. Instead of
concentrating on Jesus' prayer for unity in the Gospel of John, "unity
in organization," without taking into account the apostolic concept
of the church, is now pursued in order to arrive at world cooperation
and common action. The traditional *oikoumene* of the churches has
deteriorated into an *oikoumene* of cooperative religious societies.

But the kingdom of God and the Gospel of Jesus Christ, the
assailants of neosyncretism declare, are diametrically opposed to the
worldly pursuit of well-being and harmony of religious and secular
societies. The twentieth-century process of world development
leads clearly to an apocalyptic end and the short reign of the Anti-
christ. It is not Christ who works within the religions, the ideologies,
and the cultural, socio-political, and religious revolutions of our
time, but the spirit of the great antagonist of the Son of God. The
message of the Bible is as much in flat contradiction with the endeavors of the many nations as with the aims of a single world
church. An antitheistic humanism, elevating humanity to God,
penetrates into Christianity under the guise of a new Christian
theology, sapping the very foundations of the confessional church.

The other aspect of neosyncretism is related to the new practice of
sharing religious experiences in joint worship. At the two multireligious dialogues in Ajaltoun, Lebanon, and Colombo, Sri Lanka,
the participants shared at special occasions in each other's medita-
tions, prayers, and devotional exercises. The Ajaltoun Memorandum comments on these moments of adoration and intercession in
the following sentences:

By the very fact that we lived together, over these nine days shared our
common religious concern, and also prayed together, we were made to feel
something new, something which cannot be put into words except that we

were all too small before God, too small to dispute Him among ourselves, and that we had just to surrender, kneel down and pray. . . . Its consequence was that many of us were led to feel that we were talking too much about God?[7]

Many evangelical Christians immediately stigmatized these practices of "unified worship" as a modern form of syncretism. It is now most obvious, they declared, that the relativism and inclusiveness of Asian theology dominate the contemporary theology of missions. Not only has God in Jesus Christ become only one dimension of the manifold truth to which all others aspire in their way of spiritual concentration and devotion, but common worship is necessary to prepare all believers for the task of building up a viable and peaceful world community.

The reason these arguments are so unconvincing and weak is that they are only in appearance nourished by an explicit and glowing eschatological hope. The kingdom of God, to be sure, cannot be equated with the kingdom of this world, and the unity of the church and the unity of humanity will fully coincide only at the completion of human history. The kingdom of God will be given to humanity; no revolutionary political force, no technological planning, and not the finest religious aspirations can bring that kingdom into being. But it is quite insufficient to underline these "facts" by a series of biblical quotations and to wait for eventual positive or negative reactions to pious phrases from members of other religious communities. Attacking ecumenical Christianity with random biblical texts and announcing the days of punishment and doom, without being visibly shaken oneself by God's mighty sifting and redeeming acts, is rendering a disservice to fellow Christians and other believers alike.

Still worse, the crusaders against neosyncretism seem to suggest that it is hopeless and against God's will to struggle for a better and more human world society tomorrow. The church has apparently nothing to do but to shout God's judgment and liberation down from its rooftop into the chaotic nations and the confused religious communities of this earth. The critical remarks about "joint worship" are also misplaced because they lack the dimension of true eschatological urgency. Christians celebrating the return of their Lord in the midst of this world, that is, *in the midst* of the common life with other believers and unbelievers, have, precisely *there,* precious opportunities of giving an account of the burning hope that is in them and of interceding for the ultimate salvation of all peoples.

As long as the "we-they" mentality prevails, fears will be expressed that there is a widening gap between the ecumenical program on dialogue and the ecumenical program on mission, that also the World Council of Churches does not distinguish between legitimate and illegitimate forms of dialogue, and that dialogue serves only to create a common spirituality as a basis for a new world community. The Council will further be accused of developing the dialogue activities beyond its mandate and betraying its very own Basis. All these objections and criticisms are voiced by Christians who still cannot comprehend that the very word "mission" often includes a threat and an offense to men and women of other faiths and cultures. The term can, indeed, suggest dominance and insensitivity and frequently does not carry a connotation of human sharing in the understanding of love and responding to the truth. If one repeats that the history of Christian missions is a history of saving souls for Christ, one has great difficulty in granting other believers a right and a duty to explain their faith and to carry out their mission just as much as Christians—if the word "mission" is to be retained.

The Roman Catholic church has not abandoned a "we-they" attitude either. Following the recommendations of the Second Vatican Council, Pope Paul VI created in 1964 a Secretariat for Non-Christians and the next year a Secretariat for Non-Believers, in Rome. After a few years staff members and consultants of these two secretariats tried to change the rapidly outmoded titles of their offices but so far without success. The small word "non," they rightly protested, carries in itself condescending and pejorative connotations. "Non-Christians" and "non-believers" are in fact ridiculous expressions. Any Christian in the world would object to being called a "non-Hindu," a "non-Muslim," or a "non-Communist." (The reader may have noticed that I have used the noun or adjective "non-Christian" in quotes). As long as reference is made to others as "non-Christians" or "non-believers," the "inhabited" and the "uninhabited" world are still intentionally kept apart.

The two Vatican secretariats therefore do not function as a sincere "out-stretched hand" to religious and secular communities. Nor do they represent any challenge to the Roman Catholic church itself. As their activities are carefully controlled by the Vatican hierarchy, they are unable to move beyond traditional methods of research in the field of comparative religions and some specialized studies of modern atheism in its various expressions. The final effect of these secretariats is that they serve as an excuse for the Roman Catholic church at large to not take the entire "non-Christian" world seriously enough—by simply referring to the existence of special institutions for dialogue and the work of Christian experts who represent the church more than adequately in matters of interfaith contact and cooperation.

The World Council of Churches' Secretariat on Dialogue with People of Living Faiths and Ideologies, created in 1969, faces similar problems as the Roman Catholic secretariats, in spite of its more "up-to-date," though still rather clumsily formulated, title. Initially a department within the Division of World Mission and Evangelism, it became in 1971 a separate subunit within the Council's Programme Unit I, called "Faith and Witness." Speaking in terms of the Council's new structure it is quite significant that the "dialogue" is given a modest place within this Unit, and not in Unit II, "Justice and Service," not in Unit III, "Education and Renewal," nor in "Communications," a subunit under the Council's General Secretariat. Relations with men and women of other beliefs or ideological persuasions depend in the first place on the right interpretation of the Christian faith and a common witness, and only in the second place on an eventual worldwide working together for justice, equality, and peace, and on a possible common task in the field of political and social "conscientization." Nor can the dialogue be classified with Communications, since this subunit functions more or less exclusively as an information service to the member churches constituencies.

A Small Beginning

In spite of its structural location, the World Council's Dialogue Secretariat has made considerable progress in describing the complexity of relationships between people of various faiths and ideologies. It has repeatedly pointed to the nature of dialogue itself, stressing that dialogue is not a matter of definitions and concepts but of accepting the fact of living in dialogue, of probing into the mystery of human relations in communal contexts, and of being open to the faith of others without being less committed to one's own faith. In God's created world many people are groping in many ways for insights into the secrets of life, struggling with a faith in God beyond their power and hoping for a more human society tomorrow. Humanity is in constant labor to interpret itself and to arrive a little closer to the deciphering of its ultimate destiny. Each religious or secular community and many individuals within these communities pursue their own way of elucidating the origin, meaning, and goal of life, and with their own available resources aim at a greater degree of justice and a deeper world peace. For that very reason the dialogue, on whatever level and in whatever place, cannot be practiced as a kind of optional activity. Ecumenical Christians cannot be first of all engaged in their own affairs—matters of church unity, common witness, and joint service to the world—and also eventually add contacts and conversations with other believers or "non-believers" to their agenda. If that is the case, the dialogue remains a luxury, an exotic and not a binding affair. The World Council's constituency has also been reminded that the involvement of Christians in multireligious and ideological dialogues cannot be limited to Asia and Africa. The number of people of other faiths in Europe and America has greatly increased in recent years. In the West, too, this calls for new relationships leading to a theological reconsideration of former attitudes.

As the title of the World Council's Secretariat already suggests, dialogue deals with *people,* not with religions or ideologies as systems. It is not a discussion about dialogue, but dialogue with partners. To this should be added immediately that the dialogue cannot be confined to a few illuminated, learned, and open-minded individuals. Exchanges of religious and ideological convictions by well-informed minds and pure souls at high-level conferences tend to remain relatively harmless. At such meetings only the highest and finest ideas of the dialogue partners are singled out and reproduced in consensus statements and general resolutions to which Christians and their churches can pay little or no attention. As the last few years have shown, a long time is needed to assess critically one's own religious tradition, to share with others our inherent tendencies to dogmatism, to distinguish between authentic mission and illegitimate proselytism, and to express in concrete terms common concerns for social justice and international peace.

In order to strive after these goals a host of so-called ordinary Christians must participate in the dialogue, if the ecumenical movement at high-level conferences, in ecumenical dialogue centers, and in theological seminaries is to make further progress. Far more individual human beings in various eastern, western, and southern neighborhoods can discover that a continuous dialogue and a true desire to establish communal relationships lead to a much deeper understanding of one's own religion and to a new readiness to live our daily life face-to-face and together. Local Christians everywhere have extraordinary opportunities to express themselves in the midst of deep affinities and real divergencies, to ask radical questions about the relation between their faith and the others' faith or secular conviction, and to prepare themselves for new and transforming experiences. Ecumenical community life discloses that the intercourse between different people has not only theological but various anthropological, psychological, and sociological aspects. Far too often Christians have approached other believers or "non-believers" as abstract religious or nonreligious beings to be drawn into a stale theological argument and not to be listened to as human beings themselves, absorbed in daily work and family life, joy and sorrow, social action and individual piety.

The Secretariat on the Dialogue with People of Living Faiths and Ideologies has also stimulated theological faculties and seminaries to become more aware of the fact that the concept of "comparative study of religions," in whatever academic form, is ambiguous and should no longer be practiced as a neat theological discipline, as in the past. Since religion is always an existential involvement, it cannot be studied from the outside or at a distance. Only by living imaginatively and sympathetically within a religious culture, by knowing it from the inside, can the study be more than a merely conventional and theoretical business. Consequently, a purely intellectual and dogmatic comparison of Christianity and a "non-Christian" religion or of Christianity and Marxism—to suggest a major ideology—must be considered an unprofitable exercise. One now speaks of a theological interpretation of religions from the perspective of ultimate Christian concerns instead of a comparative study of religions. The most vital criteria of the Christian faith serve to criticize and to evaluate Christianity as much as any other world religion. If these criteria alone are used to interpret Buddhism, Hinduism, Judaism, and Islam, no narrow confessional or institutional interests have to be defended. For several years one has referred to a theology of meeting between various religions, and attempts have been made to offer models of coming together which can be pursued and studied in greater depth.

Yet the words Winfred Cantwell Smith wrote fourteen years ago still wait for a far wider echo:

I would even make bold to say that the future progress of one's own cherished faith even within one's own community depends more largely than most of us have realized on the ability to solve the question of comparative religion. Unless a Christian can contrive intelligently and spiritually to be a Christian not merely in a Christian society or a secular society but in the world; unless a Muslim can be a Muslim in the world; unless a Buddhist can carve a satisfactory place for himself as a Buddhist in a world in which other intelligent, sensitive, educated men are Christians and Muslims—unless, I say, we can together solve the intellectual and spiritual questions posed by comparative religion, then I do not see how a man is to be a Christian or a Muslim or a Buddhist at all.[8]

It is quite clear that W. C. Smith used the term "comparative religion" in the sense of a "theology and spirituality of meeting between the world religions." The real thrust of this paragraph for the ecumenical movement is that all interconfessional institutions, their staff, the churches, and individual Christians subscribing to these institutions become ecumenical only when they perform their task not merely within and for the sake of the growing Christian world community but within and for the sake of the barely visible and shaky world community. In terms of the organization of the World Council of Churches this implies that "dialogue activities" dare not remain the concern of a small subunit, demonstrating that the Council is not out of touch with other religious communities and ideological movements, but rather must provide the context and contents of "domestic" faith and order, church and society, world mission and service matters. Indeed, unless ecumenical Christianity in all its ramifications expectantly and sincerely searches for platforms and forums to tackle common religious, political, and socio-economic problems with other religious and nonreligious communities, it is difficult to see the credibility and relevance of the worldwide Christian church at all.

4

THE COMMON SEARCH
FOR COMMUNITY

In the previous chapter I alluded to the inadequacy of describing the ecumenical movement in terms of worldwide inter-religious and interideological *dialogue*. The word "dialogue" still presupposes too much a state of isolation and individual disposition on the side of the dialogue partners. People exchanging their faiths and convictions and sharing their experiences and hopes cannot afterwards simply retreat into their own spiritual, cultural, and social shells but are faced inescapably with questions of the common search for a wider and deeper community. The ecumenical movement should, therefore, be characterized in a more all-embracing sense as the search and the struggle for a "world community of communities." The term "community of communities" has to be used, of course, in an explicitly pluralistic sense. The dream of one homogeneous community and universal cosmopolitan state is a nightmare. World unity is not the universal dispersion of the human factor into the alienation of a totally planned and meaningless world. The unity of humanity can never be a totalitarian unity, an imposed uniformity. In the universal community of communities, each group should find its own place and its own identity, opting for relations of solidarity and complementarity. One has also to add immediately that the growth of world community is a long and open-ended process that cannot be defined with any precision today and steered in a fixed direction tomorrow.

It is worthwhile to note that various recent bilateral and multilateral dialogues, planned and sponsored by the World Council of

Churches' subunit on the Dialogue with People of Living Faiths and Ideologies, all center in one way or another around the theme "community." During the Ajaltoun, Lebanon, Consultation, to which I have already referred, Buddhists, Christians, Hindus, and Muslims raised questions of inter-religious dialogue on humanity and its temporal and ultimate destiny in the context of the struggle for world community. The theme of the second multilateral dialogue in Colombo, Sri Lanka, was "Toward World Community—Resources and Responsibilities for Living Together." Among several Jewish-Christian conversations, a consultation in December 1972 on the theme "The Quest for World Community: Jewish and Christian Perspectives" should be mentioned. In July of the same year a bilateral dialogue between Christians and Muslims took place at Broumana, Lebanon. The theme was "The Quest for Human Understanding and Co-operation—Christian and Muslim contributions." Another Muslim-Christian dialogue on the theme "The Unity of God and the Community of Mankind" took place at Legon, Ghana, in July 1974. Still other smaller bilateral consultations were organized to prepare for larger international gatherings in the future. The World Council's Secretariat on Dialogue also helped to formulate the third section topic of the Council's Fifth Assembly at Nairobi: "Seeking Community—The Common Search of People of Various Faiths, Cultures and Ideologies," to which I will refer in a moment. In May 1977 a major international consultation was organized by the same Secretariat in Chiang Mai, Thailand. The title of the important report, published by the World Council in the same year, was "Faith in the Midst of Faiths: Reflections on Dialogue in Community." All these ecumenical gatherings clearly indicate that the word "dialogue" has to be interpreted in the context of the search for community and the building up of a truly pluralistic world society to which small or large groups of people, in whatever place and circumstances, contribute.

In the phrase "the common search for community" a particular emphasis is placed on the word "common." The term supposes that people of various faiths, cultures, and ideologies are all increasingly caught up in social, economic, political, and environmental interdependence and challenged to seek new patterns of community in which others can fully participate. The search for definitions and

expressions of community is not an exclusively Christian preroga-
tive and task. Men and women everywhere are coming to recognize
common human aspirations and responsibilities as they are under
the same pressure in the search for justice, peace, and a hopeful
future. The quest for a more meaningful and sustaining common life
therefore raises questions about criteria for so far unknown patterns
of community and about the resources of all living faiths and
ideologies for undergirding personal and communal values.

By formulating this phrase "the common search for community"
contemporary Christianity reflects itself in a truly ecumenical mirror. It has been stated that:

true dialogue is a progressive and cumulative process, in which communities
shed their fear and distrust of each other and enter into a living together in
dialogue.[1]

Precisely such a statement urges Christians to confess—and not once
but many times—that they are sometimes afraid of being caught up
in such a process of dynamic contacts of life with life, that their desire
for security and identity in well-established Christian communities
still persists, and that they do not judge it worthwhile to be fully
open to all faiths, cultures, and ideologies of humankind. The danger remains indeed that the new phrase *"the common search for
community"* is used as an easy and cheap slogan to cover up the
inability and unwillingness to stand shoulder to shoulder with all
human beings in the quest of a wider and more embracing community. The joint affirmation that all people are increasingly caught up
in political, socio-economic, and environmental interdependence
and challenged to seek new patterns of community is contradicted
by the very fact that each religious or ideological community continues to face separately and in its own way the much divided world.

Limits to Applying Biblical Concepts and Images

Again and again the question is raised why Christians are called to
dialogue and on what ground a common search for community
should take place. Is the Christian starting point the Bible, Jesus
Christ, the church, or contemporary history and the pressure of
interdependence? Do Christians seek community through dialogue,

study, sharing, or cooperation? A majority of Christians chooses the Bible, and frequently adds the Christian tradition as the basis for dialogue and community. The Bible, to be sure, does not provide an equivalent expression for the English word "community," but it includes several Hebrew and Greek words which describe the relations between God and humanity on the one hand, and between different human beings on the other hand.

The central Old Testament term *berith* "covenant" means a "formal and solemn agreement" between God and his people. It is based upon his sovereign grace. The covenant idea excludes any notion of a union between the human and the divine. Nevertheless the covenant between God and Israel is of a close and intimate kind. According to the New Testament, a new and even deeper communion between God and humanity has been established through the life, death, and resurrection of Jesus Christ. A new and eternal covenant has been brought into being. The Greek word *koinonia* can be translated with the English words "communion" or "fellowship." Particularly in Pauline theology this concept is filled with several meanings. It is used for a fellowship between Christ and his followers as well as for the mutual fellowship of the faithful. Participation in Christ is most directly achieved and experienced in the sacrament of the Eucharist. The partaking of the bread and the wine is not merely an individual union (sharing) with the crucified and heavenly Christ. Fellowship with him necessarily leads to fellowship with all Christians, to the mutual fellowship of the members of the community. The Eucharist is constitutive of the church as the Body of Christ. The communion of the church with Christ, which is the union with the Father through him, culminates in the hope of the vision of God as he is. Present communion with God in Christ is to be consummated when the future hope of total redemption is fulfilled.

It should be quite obvious that, although the originality of the Old Testament and the New Testament teachings is a constant profound inspiration to Christians and to the world Christian community, it has no direct bearing on the meeting of Christians with people of other living faiths. Terms such as "covenant," "new covenant," *"koinonia,"* and *"agape"* are void of meaning to any person who does not or cannot believe in God's atoning and reconciling love in Jesus Christ. It is of no use to introduce these words into the theme of "seeking community together" for common reflection and discussion. As the covenant pertains to an elected people, it would be senseless to speak of God's covenant with Hindus or Muslims. It is equally meaningless to use the word *koinonia* for communal relations between Christians and Buddhists or Marxists. A *koinonia* is established only between persons who confess Jesus Christ as their Lord and Savior and believe they have been incorporated through his *agape* into his Body.

We face the same difficulties when we look at the New Testament images of the church. As is well known, the Gospels and the Epistles contain more than one hundred cognate expressions for the Christian communion. The four master images are: the people of God, the fellowship in faith, the Body of Christ, and the new creation. Other images associated with the image of "the people of God" are a "chosen race," a "holy nation," the "elect," the "holy city," and a "royal priesthood." The second major image, "the fellowship in faith," includes such cognate terms as the "sanctified," the "faithful," the "justified," the "slaves," the "household of God," the "witnessing community," and the "the sons of God." In the Pauline letters the image of the church as the "Body of Christ" is highly developed. It expresses the bonds of mutuality and solidarity accomplished in Christ's death and resurrection. Related to the concept of the Body is the concept of Christ as the head. Christ rules over the Body, sanctifies it and dies for it, and fills it with God's glory. In another major image the church is viewed by Saint Paul as the beginning of a new creation, a new humanity. Christ is the new Adam, the image of the man of heaven. The community participates in the fullness of God's glory, which is embodied in the cosmic reconciliation. Many other images of the church, such as "the salt of the earth," the "unleavened bread," the "branches of the vine," the "building on the rock," and the "bride of Christ" are also used in the New Testament.

When these images are applied to the Christian community of today, it is all too frequently forgotten that these expressions of the church grew primarily out of the revolution experienced by the speedy coming of the kingdom of God in the Messiah. "Early Christian pictures of the *world*," Paul Minear wrote,

were shaped in conformity to the Gospel. As Lord of the world, the Son of God vindicated his right to define what is world and what is church, where the world is to be found within the church and where the church within the world. Both ontologically and eschatologically the existing wall between church and world became subject to Christ's power to destroy all walls.[2]

In relation to our theme "The Common Search for Community" the serious problem is whether world Christianity is able to recover the vitality, the fluidity, and the subtlety of the New Testament images. Whether terms like "*koinonia*" and "new covenant" are used, images like "the people of God," "the new creation" are reapplied, or the classical marks of the church, namely, its oneness, holiness, catholicity, and apostolicity, are reinterpreted, old and new ecclesiologies tend to have a predominantly static, intellectualistic, and juridically minded frame of reference. Instead of looking into the eschatological future in which Christ will permanently do away with sinful human distinctions and divisions, images and doctrines of the Christian community readopt historical and institutional criteria which are backward-looking and in continuity with the past. Thus many conceptions of the church are stained with an all-too-human and sinful desire—whether this desire is overt or covert does not make any difference—to distinguish radically between the community of the faithful and communities of false believers and unbelievers, and to suggest that the separation between the one and all other communities is unalterable and permanent.

It is therefore no wonder that many Christians point out that a biblical theology of dialogical relations explaining certain structures of community between disciples of Christ and people of other faiths does not exist. The Scriptures and doctrinal theology indeed do not provide blueprints or guidelines for Christians searching for models of community with other believers or unbelievers, nor do they offer a series of notions and concepts immediately accessible and understandable to any person outside the Christian communion.

From this it does not follow, however, that an introduction and explanation of Christian ideas of community preconditions any meaningful search for wider community. It is not true that the church's experience of communion between God and his creatures and of community between human beings must be made known to all participants in the dialogue before any real conversation can start and before Christians can be ready to manifest their true desire to be an integral part of a different kind of human fellowship. But since the wish to dwell on the exclusive virtues and values of the Christian community is still so predominant—there is too little knowledge of the fact that for centuries Christianity, in spite of its numerous divisions, has been more hierarchical, complex, and monolithic in structure than all other religious communities—a vast number of Christians are reluctant, frequently even entirely unwilling, to meet others and to reflect patiently together on possible common resources for living and acting together. One is unprepared to meet without hesitation and suspicion the more mature religious and secular world. The absence of a profound eschatological anticipation and hope is the basis of a still immature Christian attitude preferring to disassociate the church in the end from the surrounding society and not to risk formulating an incomplete and untidy ecclesiology. That same attitude was characteristic also of the World Council of Churches' Fifth Assembly in Nairobi in 1975.

The Nairobi Assembly

At the beginning of this chapter I indicated that the World Council's Assembly at Nairobi discussed in the third section the theme "Seeking Community—The Common Search of People of Various Faiths, Cultures, and Ideologies." In view of the fact that such a topic was introduced for the first time into a large assembly—previous gatherings on dialogue issues were always considerably smaller and attended mostly by "specialists" in interreligious encounters—the final report of Section III can be estimated as honest and not insignificant. In the plenary section sessions as well as in the subsection sessions, a new and sharper awareness of a great urgency for seeking community beyond the Christian community became evident. "This community of ours (even if all Christians come together in one community)," the introduction of the Report stated:

has always been a minority within humanity. Our generation has become keenly aware of the religious plurality of the world. . . . We all agree that we have one solid basis, one holy reason for seeking community with others: as fellow creatures of God we are linked to each other, although in a fallen creation, sin and unbelief divide.

The presence of a few distinguished guests of other religions, explaining their beliefs, reminded the section of the reality of plurality and of the need to allow each adherent of a faith to speak his or her own language and define his or her own identity. The large group did not hesitate to assert that:

there is a necessary relationship between the local and global community. As "the new community in Christ" the Church is called upon to pre-figure that world community, but alas, the present disunity of Christians makes a mockery of that model.[3]

But for all that, the new and persistent seeking of community with others did not spill over into the other five sections. It did not arouse even slight enthusiasm in the international press. There was no feeling that a new ecumenical priority had been discovered. Objection was voiced to a preamble, later added to the document, soothing the displeasure and anger of "evangelical" Christians, who felt that the text was not sufficiently clear about the uniqueness and centrality of Christ. The opinion was heard that the report of Section III was overcautious and weak. Instead of underlining the fact that the search for community is always a confrontation in depth, never diminishes the commitment to one's own faith, is the only safeguard against syncretism, liberates from a closed system, and repudiates arrogance, the seeking of community had been touched upon in too general and uncommitted terms of cooperating together. In fact, the real depth of the richness of Christ in the living and acting together had hardly been fathomed. Other assembly participants wondered how all this penetrates into the Christian churches and changes dramatically their local habits and domestic style of life.

Ironically, the bilateral and multilateral dialogues that have taken place during the last five years confirm in part the churches' apathy toward the search for more lasting contacts with other religious families. Studying the various reports and resolutions that were the outcome of these dialogues, one is little impressed by the recommendations jointly made and the common conclusions reached. Several memoranda issued during the last few years bear the marks of vagueness, generalization, and idealism. One speaks in rather trite and conventional terms of a new approach to world community, of resources and responsibilities of living together, of a common commitment to reconstruct community, and of ways of working together. The memorandum of the multilateral dialogue at Colombo, Sri Lanka, for instance, ends with the following (I have selected six) "areas of common concern that need practical cultivation or implementation at the inter-community level": (1) promotion of social justice within and beyond political borders; (2) common concern for environmental problems that span geographical and national boundaries; (3) promotion of a strong body of opinion across all religious communities against misuse of religion to justify prejudice or hatred or warfare but rather for the right use of religion to foster brotherhood and cooperation; (4) education at many levels concerning different religious traditions, using authentic source books and jointly written or approved textbooks; (5) participation in cultural and recreational activities for all age groups in order to celebrate new experiences of community life which cut across religious and national lines; (6) support of inter-religious committees or movements dedicated to the challenging of all forms of violence.[4]

The World Conference on Religion and Peace, which so far has met twice, in Kyoto, Japan, in 1970 and in Louvain, Belgium, in 1974, issued similar vague, general, and ringing declarations. Buddhists, Christians, Confucianists, Hindus, Jains, Jews, Muslims, Shintoists, Sikhs, Zoroastrians, and still others pledged at the second conference to serve humanity together all in the way most in keeping with the convictions of their spiritual families. Governments were urged to halt the proliferation of destructive nuclear armaments and to roll back all existing nuclear weaponry until the stockpiles of nuclear devices have been safely dismantled and destroyed. All nations were asked to work for a restructuring of the world's economic system in order that a just use and distribution of raw resources, trade, and monetary policies can be achieved. The solemn gathering was convinced that its program of education for justice, peace, and universal brotherhood could be made credible.

Granted that widespread inter-religious contacts have only recently begun, that the conversations were purposely limited to the discussion of the most evident and appropriate subjects, and that all resolutions and memoranda are characterized by a peculiar style of unaccustomed and inexperienced composite authorship, one still wonders whether it is worthwhile to continue the present bilateral and multilateral dialogues. Are not all "world congresses of religion," in whatever form and under whoever's auspices, condemned to be ignored since the widening of the spirit of brotherhood, the mutual recognition of various positions, and the promotion of world justice and peace are always shattered by the hard realities of this world? Do not all representatives of world religions simply *talk* in ringing but not binding words *about* community and the building up of a world community of communities instead of earnestly examining their particular religious traditions, which are sceptical of and set limits to a common brotherhood? There would seem to be many things in favor of allowing a few high-level and regional or local dialogues to happen—it has already been shown that they are, after all, harmless and without any noticeable result—but of objecting to any serious effort to bring different religious communities together. Any true world religion is bound to draw upon its own dogmas and traditions for the formulation of its insights into community and to question, in principle, any sharing of common religious resources and any common commitment to the reconstruction of world community. None of the five world religions—Buddhism, Christianity, Hinduism, Judaism, or Islam—ever uses the term "world brotherhood" within its own constituency, and all can perceive of eternal world peace only from the unique perspective of their own divinely inspired sacred Scriptures.

Seeking Community in Calcutta

It is in the setting of Calcutta's apocalyptic society that the theme of seeking community becomes eminently real and utterly crucial. First of all, a whole series of moral imperatives and noble counsels has to be laid aside for the time being. It is quite unreal and inhuman in the Calcuttas of this world to speak of establishing good will, fostering brotherhood, respecting the dignity and worth of all human beings, participating in cultural and recreational activities, challenging all forms of violence, promoting social justice, discovering structures toward world community, and committing ourselves to reconstruct community. The Calcutta societies can never be improved, let alone renewed, unless the religious, socio-economic, and political causes of their collapse and exhaustion are firmly faced and thoroughly analyzed. No single world religion can claim that it has all the conclusive answers to the fate of millions of hungry, impoverished, and fast-dying people. Not one religious community can boast of having taken effective measures to alleviate the appalling suffering of large areas of this world. All the massive relief and aid put together is no more than a drop in the ocean of misery and despair. It would be better for the world Christian community to give up debating in conference halls whether the starting point for establishing a wider community in Calcutta is the church or Jesus Christ or the Bible. Even talk among Christians about contemporary history or human and environmental interdependence still sounds like empty words from the gallery.

Likewise, when members of various religious families come together, not much time can be spent debating whether there is indeed a "common search," a shared concern for community, communication, and culture, and what the nature of that inter-religious and intercultural community will be. The discussions cannot center around the theme of improving and developing world society, as the sheer survival of Calcutta and the whole of humanity is at stake. Calcutta is the unmistakable sign that all religious institutions have failed in their most lofty endeavors and are equally under judgment. All religious bodies have become idols by turning inward and falling prey to "community self-centeredness." They have all failed to fight successfully the demons of community, namely, self-justification, exclusiveness, self-sufficiency, and moralizing. They have all become the objects of their own worship and allegiance, laws unto themselves, and saviors of people. They have all been hiding behind millennia of old facades of religious systems and spiritual continuity.

The "achievement and maintenance of peace between the world religious families" therefore cannot be a first priority. We dare not make "the fostering of unity of peoples in society" the first point on the agenda. "Areas of common concern that need practical cultivation or implementation at the intercommunity level" cannot be calmly discussed at dignified inter-religious gatherings. In the topsy-turvy society of Calcutta where Hindus, Muslims, Buddhists, Jains, Sikhs, Christians, and Jews finally can meet, the common search for community is a most delicate, painful, and provisional enterprise. The search is delicate because, precisely in Calcutta, the establishment of a community based on greater justice is not achieved by friendly dialogue and wide reconciliation but by a hard confrontation of opposing groups and by violent revolution. I will discuss this aspect of viable community in the next chapter. The common search is painful because no religious group can maintain that it has reached into the depth of its faith and lived in obedience to its divine laws and precepts. And the common search is provisional because all religions are characterized by specific "eschatological" perspectives on community. Their ultimate outlooks imply a critique of any human community and transcend every limitation of human community and views of communities. Consequently current inter-religious dialogues have to move away from a dangerous activism and a superficial optimism about possibilities and responsibilities for the development of world community. An enumeration of ethical common denominators and a mutual encouragement to work together for a greater justice, equality, and peace will hardly enhance that world community. Every kind of search for some cheap and external form of community is not only of no benefit but is even an abomination to Calcutta societies. Such societies exist to test the legitimacy of the ultimate hopes and visions of genuine community, nurtured within world religions. If these visions and hopes do not truly transcend the best and the worst mundane societies, they had better be discarded as deceptive and illusory.

Facing Calcutta's perplexing dilemmas and its lack of any sustaining community life, devout Buddhists must re-examine whether the sole cause of suffering is indeed, according to the second noble truth, the thirst (*tanha*) leading to rebirth, the craving of passions, and the craving for existence. Does the eightfold path, namely, right understanding, right thought, right speech, right bodily action, right livelihood, right effort, right mindfulness, and right concentration, lead indeed to total freedom? Can one hope for Nirvana only if one has achieved perfect self-control, unselfishness, knowledge, and enlightenment? Are millions of street dwellers to be admonished to start the road to a passionless peace? Devout Hindus have to ponder again their belief that *Brahman* as the holy power pervades and sustains the outer world while *atman* (the eternal self) is surrounded but untouched by the most debasing material conditions and powers. Can *bhakti,* the contemplative attitude of loving adoration toward Siva and Vishnu, or yoga, culminating in the synthesis and identification of *Brahman* and *atman* (*tat tvam asi*) be practiced by endless crowds of sick and starving human beings? Even if life can be conceived as a cyclical process, in which the eternal soul passes through a long series of successive bodies, is it true that there is no memory of previous birth as the self is deprived of its sensory and intellectual faculties between one life and the next? Can Calcutta's horrors so easily be written off? Do they just serve to keep the cycle of true life (*samsara*) going until the self will achieve *moksa* or liberation?

Devout Muslims have to elucidate more fully that the God who revealed himself to the Prophet was one who created everything from nothing and shows in his daily guidance the continued activity of his creative power. Does the commitment to a sense of humanity's utter dependence on Allah justify a certain detachment and concern in the face of all dangers and adversities, ascribing all events to his power and to his mysterious and almighty nature? Can the clearly defined set of moral teachings of the Qur'an, leading to a balanced synthesis of law and spirit, so readily be applied to the highly entangled and tormented society of Calcutta? The Qur'an says that "he who is blind in this life will be blind in the life after death, and will find himself even more astray" (17:73). How does this ethical legalism, rewarding the good and punishing the bad, square with the hellish predicament of more than one-third of humankind, even if it is admitted that the pains and torments after this life—can they be more intense than in Calcutta?—will come to an end and all humanity will ultimately find admission to the grace and mercy of God.

Devout Jews will have to ask themselves again: is Israel's task not ultimately more than to fulfill and to bring God's Holy Law to the nations, preserving its particularity and exclusiveness as God's chosen people at all costs? Are not particularity and universality mutually contradictory despite their affirmation that particularity is a universal empirical fact and universalism is a particular goal of Israel's singular monotheism? Is not even Israel unable to achieve sanctification of life as the Lord himself will make a new covenant with his people and write his law on their hearts (Jer. 31: 31–34)? Does not the prophecy of the suffering servant (Isa. 53:1–12), a text unheeded and left to Christianity for its interpretation, speak far more directly to the afflicted, the despised, and the disfigured? How will the nations one day worship the one and only God on Mount Zion when whole societies are literally falling apart and doomed to annihilation?

It would be better for devout Christians, as for all other believers, to begin by being perturbed and silent in the world's Calcuttas. What are their credentials to speak of God's love and justice? Who is taken into God's new covenant? Is not the Christian *koinonia* an oasis in the desert? How do all others fit into God's all-embracing plan of salvation? The cross of Jesus Christ is certainly also erected in Calcutta. But how can ecumenical Christians witness to the death and resurrection of their Lord otherwise than in terms of the catholicity of the church, their call to world mission, and their extensive aid to increasingly impoverished countries? What really binds Christians everywhere and Calcutta's street dewellers together?

The theme "Seeking Community—The Common Search of People of Various Faiths, Cultures and Ideologies" has been introduced as a new concern and task by the ecumenical movement. But will it remain on its agenda? On the one hand, the slow building up and the growth of a world community of communities seems to correspond to some high aspirations of humanity's religions. Representatives of Christianity and various religious families testify today to the necessity of a common search for community. But on the other hand, the quest for world community is still bedeviled by mutual exclusion and suspicion and could well cease tomorrow. Will all world religions then be thrown back into the long period of hostility, competition, aggressive mission, and proselytism? Only Calcutta can teach each religious group that the contemporary search for world community must never become the instrumentality for activist eschatological realization. Calcutta's situation is far too desperate for world religions together to give its inhabitants hope. Confronted with its vast crowds, each religion can only point in great humility and with much self-restraint to the achievement of the *eschaton* which is the essential core of its faith and the only effective motivation of its conduct. Only the deepest common hope that humanity will find its ultimate destiny can shorten the wide span of world history and cut through the cycle of eternal rebirth. One can speak of a common search for world community only if the very last hopes are profoundly tested against each other and lived out by each group of the faithful in ever greater depth.

5

CHRISTIAN SOCIAL ETHICS
VIS-À-VIS MARXIST IDEOLOGY

In the previous chapters, terms such as "ideology," "contemporary ideologies," "secular community," and "interideological dialogue" have been used without further explanation or definition. Referring a few times to the World Council of Churches' Sub-unit on Dialogue with People of Other Faiths and Ideologies, I have limited myself to the recent history and ecumenical evaluation of inter-religious dialogues and to the meeting of various religious communities, not taking into account the confrontation of world religions with twentieth-century ideologies and the place of secular communities within the world community of communities. Among current ideologies, we have now to mention liberal capitalist ideology, social democratic ideology, Marxist ideology, nationalism, technocratism, reactive ideologies, and cultural traditionalism.

In this chapter I will deal mainly with socialist and Marxist-Leninist ideologies and with revolutionary ideological governments. It will be seen that world Christianity has not only not yet succeeded in clarifying its position vis-à-vis various models of socialism but has also made very little progress in analyzing its own deliberate or unconscious ideological positions. The Roman Catholic church, other churches, and the World Council of Churches have, until today, refused to endorse any concrete choice between a neoliberal socio-political system and a socialist ideology in a given historical context. There is no doubt that in this respect especially, the churches and their ecumenical movement have to be steered beyond past and present reflections and ventures. The urgency of opting for a consistent, practicable, and coherent ideology, breaking down class barriers, distributing national wealth more equally, and assuring greater social justice becomes even more evident when we look again at the hopeless plight of the Fourth World. We will start by surveying briefly the history of the Christian encounter with the concept of ideology and ideological movements.

The Last Forty Years

From the thirties to the sixties the term "ideology" in Christian social theology was used in an exclusively pejorative sense. Ideologies, and particularly revolutionary ideologies of Marxist origin, were regarded as total systems of thought competing for the spiritual allegiance of humanity. As they are based on utter godlessness, the consequence of distorted social perspectives and surrender to utopian expectations, they must be unequivocally rejected. The Second World Conference on Church and Society at Edinburgh (1937) stated:

Every tendency to identify the Kingdom of God with a particular structure of society or economic mechanism must result in moral confusion for those who maintain the system and in disillusionment for those who suffer from its limitations.[1]

A year later the Tambaram Conference of the International Missionary Council expressed itself as follows:

Marxist communism in its orthodox philosophy stands clearly opposed to Christianity. It is atheistic in its conception of ultimate reality and materialistic in its view of man and his destiny. Its utopian philosophy of history lacks the essential Christian notes of divine judgement, divine governance and eternal victory. This revolutionary strategy involves the disregard of the sacredness of personality which is fundamental to Christianity. The challenge it presents should deepen our conviction that, whatever one's social philosophy, the Christian faith alone gives the vision and power that are essential for the basic solution of the problems of our troubled world.[2]

In his Encyclical Letter *Divini Redemptoris* Pope Pius XI condemned communism more strongly than any twentieth-century ecumenical gathering. Quoting Pope Leo XIII, who defined communism as "the fatal plague which insinuates itself into the very marrow of human society only to bring about its ruin," he warned all the faithful that "communism is intrinsically wrong, and [that] no one who would save Christian civilization may collaborate with it in any undertaking whatsoever."[3]

The contribution of the first two assemblies of the World Council of Churches to the ecumenical analysis of ideologies carried the argument in a new direction. At Amsterdam (1948) the churches were admonished "to reject the ideologies of both Communism and *laissez-faire* capitalism," seeking "to draw men away from the false assumption that these extremes are the only alternatives." The idea of the "responsible society" was proposed as an alternative to such ideological extremes and as a way of seeking "creative solutions which never allow either justice or freedom to destroy the other."[4] The Evanston Assembly, reflecting cold war experiences, reiterated the main points of the First Assembly on the conflict between Christian faith, Marxist ideology, and totalitarian practice. It also pointed however, for the first time to the unfortunate effects that sterile anticommunism was producing in many western societies. Nevertheless, until 1966 it was repeated several times that Christians must say a very clear no to the communist state before they can begin to recognize positive aspects within the communist achievement. The churches must work to enlarge the area of freedom through "gradual and slow" reform.

At the World Conference on Church and Society in Geneva in 1966, ideologies like communism were for the first time approached in a largely new nonwestern world context. The Conference succeeded in defining ideology in a nonpejorative sense:

By ideology we mean a process quite different from a total system of ideas which is closed to correction and new insight. Ideology as we use it here is the theoretical and analytical structure of thought which undergirds successful action to realize revolutionary change in society or to undergird and justify its *status quo*. Its usefulness is proved in the success of its practice. Its validity is that it expresses the self-understanding, the hopes and values of the social group that holds it, and guides the practice of that group.

This new, positive understanding of ideology reflected the concern to open Christian thought to new ideological developments arising in the liberation struggles in Africa, Asia, Latin America, and the Middle East. The gathering in Geneva admitted that:

theology reflects not only action but interaction between God's revelation and man's ideological understanding of his own condition and desires. Christians, like all other human beings, are affected by ideological perspectives.[5]

The Council's Department on Church and Society, organizing in 1970 an exploratory conference on the subject "Technology and the Future of Man and Society," went on to say that "the relation of faith to ideology remains a question to be worked out in concrete situations."[6]

As this whole problem had to be inserted officially somewhere into the World Council's program, the Central Committee at Addis Ababa in 1971 decided to add the two words "and Ideologies," to the phrase "Dialogue with People of Other Faiths." By doing so, it indicated that the outreach of dialogue should include the proponents of both religious and ideological worldviews. No suggestions or recommendations, however, were made as to how to work out a combined dialogue between religions and ideologies or even a bilateral Christian-Marxist dialogue. While it was right not to put ideologies in a totally different category—because religions in dialogue are apt to defend their common religious front against a threatening secular world, and because all religions tend to deny forcefully any ideological infiltration or bias within their own systems of faith—the follow-up of the 1971 mandate resulted in a twofold embarrassment.

On the one hand, a small Christian-Marxist consulation sponsored by the Department on Church and Society in 1968 remained a single and isolated event. The impossibility of finding Eastern European Marxists and communists from Asia, Africa, and Latin America willing to participate in an ongoing and meaningful dialogue was repeatedly emphasized. The old questions were also still raised as to what the purpose of such a dialogue is, what specific issues are to be discussed, and what method of approach at the ecumenical level should be recommended. On the other hand, in spite of a more positive ecumenical view of ideology in theory and practice, one of the conclusions of the 1966 Church and Society Conference remained valid:

> there is no agreement among Christians themselves on the degree to which analysis and action in Christian ethics itself must wrestle with ideological bias.[7]

Thus the World Council of Churches continued to wonder how to face the task of defining the term "ideology" more precisely for its own use and of undertaking some conclusive studies of ideological presuppositions and perspectives implicit in the formulation and implementation of a number of its programs and activities.

Several years later the World Council's Central Committee, meeting in Berlin in 1974, looked again into the whole problem of ideology and ideologies and made the following recommendations: (a) "to propose an alternative terminology," as "ideology" ambiguously refers "to a constructive vision for social change or to an idolatrous system," (b) to ask "how far ideological presuppositions may be contributing to the unity or disunity of the Church," and (c) to find "appropriate ways to support Christians for whom ideologies represent a threat rather than a positive challenge."[8] This mandate was followed up by an "Ecumenical Consultation on Faith and Ideologies" held at Cartigny, near Geneva, in May 1975. The memorandum issued by this exploratory conference was a general and defensive domestic document, in no way related to the actual ideological struggles and hard clashes in all parts of the world. By adopting the neutral usage of the term "ideology" as "an expression—systematic or not—of human views of social reality which reflect the basic conditions of the life of social groups," the process of dealing concretely with ideologies was reversed and pushed back into the period before the Geneva Church and Society Conference.

The main concern of the Cartigny meeting was "to see how Christians of different ideological commitments can live together in the 'space for confrontation in Christ' without turning diversity into hostility." The participants were therefore quite satisfied with raising the questions of how the unity of the church is affected by the diverse ideological commitments of Christians in different parts of the world and what the limits are beyond which diversity may break the fellowship of the church. Not the theoretical and analytical structure of ideological reflection undergirding successful action to realize social change but the integrity and continuity of the worldwide Christian community were the backbone of the discussion. By repeating once more that "ideological expressions have religious implications . . . in so far as they make statements of ultimate significance about human nature, society and history and demand total commitment,"[9] the Consultation ignored the fact that, as an integral part of contemporary society, ideology can provide an opportunity for self-understanding and serve as a dynamic factor in social change. Only a few were concerned that the common task is not to "prove" that the ecumenical fellowship can comprehend various ideological encounters, but to emphasize that in many present situations the elaboration of an efficacious ideology, creating a new conscious and critical infrastructure of society, is a matter of Christian discipleship and obedience. From this it does not follow at all that a concrete ideological commitment must be interpreted as a total religious commitment.

The Nairobi Assembly was not able to carry the debate on ideology and on the seeking of community with ideological groups and parties a step further. Participants in the third subsection of Section III frankly admitted that they were not well prepared to discuss such an unusual and difficult topic. Much time was spent on a suitable working agenda, on the questions of whether socialism (in contrast to communism) is an ideology (and not rather a movement), and whether ideological coexistence is possible. When a Bulgarian and a Russian delegate expounded the view that Christianity is not an ideology but that nevertheless the church and the state in their countries are in continual dialogue, an African participant asked whether the Christian faith has no ideological consequences, what the daily subjects of the dialogue are, and whether the church practices coexistence because of its faith or out of necessity for sheer survival. Another African Christian, impressed by the speeches of his Eastern European colleagues on religious freedom in their countries and on the churches' manifestation of solidarity with their governments' social policies, posed the question whether the Russian model of communism, which apparently so successfully corresponded to the aspirations and needs of all citizens, should not more widely be adopted by African nations.

Only one voice pointed out that the church is directly confronted with institutional ideology. As Christendom stood for a long time on the wrong side of society, ideology had to be embodied in concrete societal structures. For that very reason Christians today, the participant concluded, are still fearful of the word "ideology" and do not know how to reply to the challenge of institutional Marxism. Section III was unable to make any specific proposals to search for possible forms of community between Christians and Marxists, just as Section V, dealing with "Structures of Injustice and Struggles for Liberation," and Section VI, discussing "Human Development, Ambiguities of Power, Technology, and Quality of Life," ignored the necessity of dealing with an ideological analysis of society and an ideological commitment to the change of social structures, and the need to face the achievements and victories of Marxist-orientated governments. Before trying to assess the lack of content in present Christian social theology vis-à-vis Marxist ideology, I would like to insert a few pages here on the history of the Christian-Marxist dialogue and to explain why this dialogue, flourishing during the late fifties and the sixties, lost its steam and impact in the 1970s.

The Christian-Marxist Dialogue

The dialogue started in France and Italy. On the Marxist side stood R. Garaudy, G. Mury, L. Lombardo-Radice, C. Luporini, and several other philosophers who had become major spokesmen. On the Christian side the Fathers Dubarle, Jolif, Chenu, and Girardi, the Protestant professors of theology G. Casalis, A. Dumas, J. Bosc, and others participated in many meetings. The *Paulus-Gesellschaft* sponsored four international conferences in Austria and Germany (in Salzburg, Herrenchiemsee, Marienbad, and Bonn). K. Rahner, J. B. Metz, J. Y. Calvez, and M. Reding were among the participants. The dialogue in Czechoslovakia was led by J. Hromadka and his disciples J. M. Lochman, J. Smolik, and M. Opcensky. On the Marxist side M. Machovec, V. Gardavsky, M. Prucha, and E. Kadlecova showed high intelligence and sensitivity. The works of the Polish Marxists A. Schaff and L. Kolakowski became widely known. In Yugoslavia several public dialogues were organized. *Praxis* became a leading journal for Christian-Marxist discussion. In Great Britain J. Klugmann, an editor of *Marxism Today*, and P. Oestreicher, a staffmember of the British Council of Churches, edited two books on the Christian-Communist dialogue in their country. R. Garaudy visited the United States several times, and symposia were held at a number of American universities. P. Lehmann, H. Cox, R. L. Shinn, L. Dewart, J. L. Adams, and others devoted a series of articles to the ongoing dialogue. By 1969 more than twelve hundred books, pamphlets, and periodical essays in English, French, German, Spanish, and Italian on the Christian-Marxist dialogue had been published, an extraordinary explosion of literature in less than ten years.

Among the many issues and problems debated at various gatherings one can list atheism, death, transcendence, alienation, Christian and Marxist eschatology, the individual and the community, free will and determinism, a common search for the meaning of life, and Christian and Marxist standards of morality. There is no doubt that the confrontations and conversations resulted in the elimination of various prejudices, misunderstandings, and false interpretations of each other's position.

Marxists openly admitted that religion is not always the "opium of the people" and that particularly Christianity has been at some moments in history, and still can be, a protest against an unjust society and against exploitation and oppression in this world. Christians were welcomed by communists in the struggle for a socialist society. Marx himself, many Marxist dialogue partners reiterated, was never a militant atheist, because the essence of atheism in his works was not a no to religion and God, but a yes to the world and the mastery of human life and history. The Marxist workers' movement therefore was not inspired by a theoretical denial of God, but its atheism resulted from the necessity to fight against an apolitical Christianity and political clericalism. The road to the self-liberation of the proletariat could be travelled only apart from the church.

R. Garaudy repudiated the Christian notion of transcendence in the following statement:

A rejection of transcendence means a refusal to turn into an answer what is merely a question, a refusal to turn a need into a presence. To affirm transcendence means to deny that man is able to realize himself fully in this empirical life. . . . Marxism insists upon the awareness that man is never completed. . . . Marxist dialectic is as rich in its awareness of the infinite and as demanding as Christian transcendence . . . . It is even richer, because if nothing is promised to us and nobody waits for us, man's responsibility is a total one. The meaning which he gives to history depends only on himself.[10]

Several Marxists also assured Christians that socialism is by no means a magical leap from an alienated to a dealienated society. As the contradictions of social life cannot be liquidated in some final act of liberation, communists must constantly criticize all forms of de-humanizing tendencies and seek radical change as a fermenting factor in even advanced socialist societies. Communism cannot be seen as an absolute goal in the sense that compared with it everything else becomes a mere means to an end, or in the sense that it will be the final stage for humankind. In the matter of the decay and death of religion in a socialist society, several Marxists confirmed their con-viction that religion will not simply wither away. The roots of reli-gion do not lie in the antagonism of economic interests and cannot be reduced to political and social relationships. Precisely in a socialist society, deeper alienations of the human self will come to the forefront and religion will continue to transcend the world according to its essence. As long as the fear of death continues to exist, they submitted, the wish for immortality and thus also for religion will exist.

Christian partners in the dialogue pointed out that Feuerbach's mistake was not to proclaim that God is an idea of humanity, but to ignore that God is a *necessary* idea of humanity. It is inherent in human nature to seek beyond the tangible. Concerning the question of an open future it was stressed on various occasions that Christian eschatology cannot be equated with a mere passive expectation of the hereafter or a hope of immortality for the individual soul. Sound biblical eschatology is always creatively and responsibly connected with the well-being of contemporary society. Salvation—an excel-lent and perfected humanity—is not lying beyond us, but before us, and does not descend from heaven to us, but is ever approaching us. The Christian hope for an absolute future protects humanity against the temptation to manipulate the future of this world by brutally sacrificing one generation to the other for the sake of a utopian classless society that can never be totally realized. The best human society does not make the Gospel superfluous. On the contrary, in the best socialist society new questions will not find answers, and the

Christian faith will respond to new disillusions and perplexities. Some Christians also expressed the hope that communism will eventually break away from atheism as there is an inner conflict between the definition of itself as a rational, historical form of thought and its messianic claim to absolutism.

Christians in the dialogue further deplored the churches' primitive anticommunist attitude. Recognizing atheism as a major phenomenon of our secular era, they pledged to help the church to refrain from holy crusades against the unbelieving world. Faith, they repeatedly stated, is no assured possession to be shown off against atheistic fellow men and women. Concerning the participation of Christians in class struggle and the revolutionary overthrow of oppressive regimes, the question was raised as to the extent to which Christians can cooperate with Marxists without embracing communism as the only true form of human society. Many other topics were discussed, and many other opinions and convictions, leading to further questioning and mutual understanding, were expressed.

Just as the dialogue progressed rapidly and successfully and was followed in wider circles of Christian and Marxist learning, so too did it swiftly decline after the 1968 invasion of the Soviet army in Czechoslovakia. The term "Christian-Marxist dialogue," which still aroused interest, excitement, and hope even a few years ago, is often used now in a pejorative sense of academic conversations of "pure souls" at high level meetings unrelated to political struggle and ideological praxis. For many, especially among the younger generation, in the southern as well as in the northern hemispheres, both Marxism and the church are nothing but "ugly old ladies," or "old hats." The U.S.S.R. has, so they say, betrayed the revolution by becoming a bourgeois power just as the church and western democracy continue to betray Christ by not actively changing the status quo of society. Both the East-West tension and the East-West dialogue are antiquated and immaterial issues. The world is not divided between Christians and Marxists, but between exploiters and exploited.

As the Christian-Marxist dialogue took no notice of China and the liberation struggles in Latin America and Africa, it has now been superseded by theologies of liberation and socialist revolution in an authentic Third World context. The Russian model of socialism inspires only a few countries outside the Atlantic community. According to several Third World nations and many individuals in the West, it is Maoism that has given the example of how many millions of formerly exploited, degraded, and hungry people can feed themselves today, lead a sober, industrious, and dignified life, care for each other from infancy to old age, and be united in common goals, including nation building, security for all, and support of peoples' liberations in many countries. True Christians and Marxists in the underdeveloped world have no time and cannot afford the luxury of discussing together transcendence, atheism, eschatology, the different premises of Christian and Marxist anthropology, and the creative interplay between humanism and naturalism. Consequently they do not consider themselves partners in a friendly and intelligent Christian-Marxist dialogue, but press on together to fight structures of domination and injustice upheld by reactionary governments, political parties, and multinational firms seeking expansion, profit, and stability at any cost. Third World people speak of the Christian-Marxist dialogue in a reversed sense. It is not an intellectual dialogue that leads them to cooperation. Instead, historical conditions prompt them to common action, and it is within the joint struggle that their dialogue continues. The movement "Christians for Socialism," which started in 1972 in Chile and spread to a number of South American and European countries, endorses much of what I have reported above.

There is another major reason why the European Christian-Marxist dialogue had such a short life. The dialogue had no influence on the basic attitude of the churches in the West and was never accepted by the churches in the East since quiet and neutral coexistence is still the standard Christian strategy for meaningful survival in intolerant socialist states. Many Christians in the West continue to assert that ideologies are too simplistic to be relevant in advanced and complex societies. In fact, ideologies are not only irrelevant, they believe, but harmful. Fanaticism and totalitarianism are automatically added to the definition of ideology. Only a minority in the United States and Great Britain admit that their countries, which are considered to be the most pragmatic ones in the world, have deep ideological roots. One of the fundamental ideas underlying American society, it is correctly pointed out, is the ringing assertion

in the Declaration of Independence that all men are created equal—
a thoroughly ideological statement.

The dialogue between Marxists and Christians also failed really to
challenge the ecumenical movement. The World Council of
Churches was not keen to face more fully the claims, implications,
and consequences of Marxist ideology. Its last official statement on
communism dates back to its Second Assembly in 1954. The Evanston statement was not only general and prudent but a typically
evasive response to the international situation of bilateral
American-Russian tension. The People's Republic of China, established in 1949, has never been explicitly mentioned at any major
ecumenical conference. Only the Uppsala Assembly stated in a few
sentences some concern for the admission of China into the United
Nations. At the last Assembly of the East Asia Christian Conference
at Singapore in 1973, where its title was changed to the Christian
Conference of Asia, a single sentence, which would "recognize the
profound achievement of the People's Republic of China in reform-
ing its society and in promoting the welfare of its people," was voted
down by a vast majority of delegates who stated: "We do not know
enough about China," "we are not a political organization, but a
religious group," "we as Christians cannot approve of a communist
regime."[11] All these old arguments were heard again in opposition to
a simple recognition of an alternative system, where one of the
primary targets is the overcoming of acquisitiveness, greed, and
selfishness.

The dialogue hardly changed the fundamental Marxist attitude
toward Christianity, either, and never penetrated into the Communist parties of Eastern and Western European countries. As before, any faith in a personal God who reveals himself is rejected as an
impoverishment of humanity and a depreciation of human autonomy. Dialogue for communists is finally only a means of enlisting
as many individual Christians as possible in the battle for socialism.
The western institutional churches have to be classified as enemies
of the communist cause and must be entirely written off. Churches
in the East are tolerated as long as they proclaim to support the
building up of the socialist state but are never considered an integral
part of public and social life. There is also a clear trend among the
Marxist dialogue partners, now all expelled as "revisionists" from

their Communist parties, toward a new utopian socialism. The problem of alienation has been detached from the classical distinction between the "infra and supra structure." Alienation today is not caused so much by private ownership and exploitation of the proletariat by the bourgeois class as by the oppressive and clumsy bureaucracy of the state system. Marxist dialectics are replaced by cybernetics aiming at a chiliastic realm of freedom. And atheism is covered up by a new kind of Hegelian pantheism, which is equally to be rejected by the Christian faith.

Communist parties and governments, when by chance informed of it, are suspicious of a progressive Christian social ethics which advocates rather radical changes in various liberal Christian Democratic systems and condemns societies ruled by a military dictatorship. They cannot understand how Christians can speak of the blessing of secularization, a modern process in which God has been discarded as a working hypothesis and humanity has come of age. They are confused that the World Council of Churches sponsors a program to combat racism that contains covert or overt subversive ingredients. They do not quite grasp that there are Christians in many countries holding up the banner "Christians for Socialism." Did not Marx say that religion is the opium of the people and did not Lenin speak of opium for the people? Are the Christian churches not busy as before organizing their anticommunist campaigns? Can one ever seriously count on Christian participation in preparing for a revolution and carrying out that revolution to its bitter end? Can the Christian individualistic approach to human society, which sets out from individuals and their selfishness and corrects them for the sake of the community and social justice, ever be reconciled with the communist approach, which sets out from the ideal of the community and social justice and makes concessions to individuals and their egoism?

Many other questions could be added. One thing, however, is sure: whether Christian or communist, neither knows what to make of the phrase "the world community of communities." Peaceful coexistence is a hypocritical and deceitful idea as the one only hopes to triumph over the other. Our twofold conclusion is that the Christian-Marxist dialogue failed, on the one hand, because it indulged in lofty reflections and in pronouncements on paper instead of suggesting concrete and direct actions to serve the helpless and suffering neighbor, and on the other hand, and even more so, because both the churches and the communist nations continued to look at each other as foes, forced to compete with one another in the struggle for a better society. Christians were as much drawn back to their church as Marxists were reimprisoned in their Communist parties, in spite of all their respective institutional criticisms. It is a difficult guess whether the Christian identification and solidarity with the millions whom Christ calls the least of his brothers and sisters are marked by a greater authenticity than the communist identification and solidarity with the worldwide proletariat, which still desperately seeks a united international front.

Because of recent political developments in Italy, Portugal, and Spain, the Christian-Marxist dialogue received a new impetus. For example, the Communist Party of Italy (CPI), desiring to discuss cooperation between Christians and communists in Italy as well as in other European countries, participated in a conference which took place in Florence in the fall of 1975. Not only representatives from West Germany, Austria, and Yugoslavia but also from Canada and the United States were present. The meeting was organized by the *Paulus-Gesellschaft,* which had not been active for several years. A European congress of Christians and Marxists was held at Salzburg, Austria, in the fall of 1977. The *Paulus-Gesellschaft* sponsored another symposium at Düsseldorf in August 1978. The theme was "Marxist Philosphy and Christian Values Today." Although these new initiatives to more widely discuss ideological options and political cooperation are to be welcomed, and although a critical attitude toward the Soviet Union is evident—CPI committeeman Luciano Gruppi bluntly spoke of the Soviet system as a "proletarian dictatorship with bureaucratic deformations"—the renewed Christian-Marxist dialogue still tends to be an intra-European debate, ignoring the socialist ideologies that are taking shape in the Third World. Obviously, Communist parties in the countries of southern Europe cannot afford to alienate Catholics; and obviously Christians cannot ignore the leftist electoral victories. But unless matters of working together are shared in a much more international ideological context, it does not make much difference "what kind of a meal is cooked in the European kitchen." Concrete solidarity with the exploited and impoverished world must be a yardstick, as I said before, for national ideological choices and political decisions.

Christian Situation Ethics

It is quite clear, particularly after this short survey of the rise and decline of the Christian-Marxist dialogue, that the last forty years of Christian social ethics and the manifold ecumenical stimuli to worldwide action still strongly condition Christianity's socio-political outlook today. Although it is no longer stipulated that the task of the churches and of individual Christians is to work for a "Christian civilization" or a "Christian social order" bearing the distinctive marks of a Christian understanding of humanity and society, the thesis is still much defended that "the Christian faith alone gives the vision and power that are essential for the basic solution of the problems of this world." Christians, knowing that no single social structure can be identified with the kingdom of God, and that no political struggle between the proletarian class and the bourgeois class will ever lead to a classless society, can claim to be protected against the totalitarian passion, the moral confusion, and the unexpected disillusionment of leftist regimes. Their faith enables and encourages them to continue to struggle for justice, freedom, and equality through more gradual and less violent or even peaceful social reforms. The "principles" of the "middle axioms" have to be constantly redefined so that Christians may live "critically" and "responsibly" in diverse societies. The churches must be on their guard not "to take too much initiative" in defining a "too definite shape" of a particular human society. All this can be characterized as "Christian situation ethics," which helps the churches to orientate themselves in the confusing and complicated battles of this world. But this kind of social ethics neither faces the intensely ideological battles which have to be fought nor does it openly recognize the very existence of zealous secular societies committed to the practical implementation of a particular ideology.

Christian situation ethics is therefore unsatisfactory and incomplete when directly confronted with the question of competing or cooperating with socialist or even revolutionary communist regimes. Even if a majority of churches were to agree in defining "ideology" in a positive context, for instance, as a set of dynamics expressing the interests of social groups with the purpose of changing the social structure, a valid evaluation of ideological concerns would not be undertaken. Such a definition would imply only that Christians should denounce a traditional alienating and mystifying infrastructure and help others to step back from a given system of oppression and enslavement. There would be no suggestion whatever that Christians should be ready to participate in the elaboration of a substitute ideology, which could create a new conscious and critical infrastructure of society. Even less would such a definition imply that Christians can and should assure the effective transformation of the old society by taking active part in the more or less violent overthrow of the old oppressive regime. History has shown that so far Christians have hardly been in the forefront of guerrilla warfare and a communist revolution. Camilo Torres remains a very great exception. Out of a special fund the World Council's Programme to Combat Racism has made contributions to organizations and liberation movements which are themselves victims of racism. Money has been given with one condition: that it be used only for humanitarian programs. The World Council of Churches has never made an appeal to join the armed forces of liberation movements. Of course, all Christians are encouraged to work for social change because social justice demands it. But the endorsement of a specific revolutionary ideology and the participation in revolutionary struggle aiming at the overturn of a status quo government is left entirely to the individual conscience.

As all revolutions quickly grow old and as there is no guarantee that the new, ruling class will not misuse its political power and turn itself into a repressive, corrupt, and self-perpetuating regime, a Christian social ethics is, moreover, obliged to keep the two dimensions of ideology, namely, ideology as bias or social illusion and ideology as truth or social insight, carefully apart. Power structures that remain unchallenged and unchecked easily fall a victim to totalitarianism and extreme self-righteousness. This risk is particularly great when the established social system is defended solely in the name of humanity's eminent capacity to ensure justice and to promote a greater humanization of society. The demons of party monopoly and state absolutism in every realm of life can only be exorcised by a sound and critical theology. Here, of course, world-wide orientated Christianity fulfills its task. On several occasions it has affirmed that the Gospel transcends all ideologies and that the acknowledgment of the lordship of Jesus Christ challenges the in-grown tendency of the human race to give particular patterns of socio-economic organization a religious sanction which they do not deserve. The lack of the knowledge of God as the judge of human history is at the root of all ideological and totalitarian triumphalism.

The continuous revitalization of theology vis-à-vis ideology is indeed of paramount importance to contemporary Christendom. Unfortunately it is frequently overlooked that theology, just like ideology, is always in danger of playing the role of a competitor. Updating theology by adding a number of qualifying nouns—during this last decade catchwords like a "theology of revolution," a "theology of secularization," a "theology of liberation," a "theology of development" were coined—comes close to preserving the rele-vance of theology at all costs. In subscribing to these theologies the churches seem to keep up with history and to deal critically with humanity's ambiguous efforts to build the city of God. But they do not realize that by pleading God's cause they have taken his place and have deprived the Gospel of its savor, its risk, and its promise. They forget that the Christian faith is not a faith in an idea, nor in what is behind reality, but in God's dealing with human history. In analyzing a political or ideological situation "in the light of the Gospel," that is, from their own transcendental point of view, they end up hovering over the political and ideological conflicts. By seemingly transcending their own ideological commitments they have modified theology to a dangerous status quo ideology.

The other, not less real, danger is that Christian social theology stay in the realm of "geographical" description of social circum-stances, diligently practice Christian exhortation, and provide no more than guidelines for limited ad hoc common actions in emer-gency situations. There is not sufficient awareness that Chris-tian ethics has to deal with thorough historical analysis and painstak-ing historical mediation in any given society. Christian openness to oppression and exploitation and Christian indignation about in-equality and injustice, motivated by the faith that God in Christ took upon himself the whole burden of human wickedness and weakness, do not serve as adequate responses to the sinful facts of human history. Scientific instruments for analyzing the real dynamics of society and assessing the churches' role in that society are more than ever indispensable. Still today the articulation of Christian love is often too haphazard, even sentimental, and falls prey to the secular self-interests of those who are in power. True knowledge for intelligent and effective action can be acquired only by starting from the concrete predicaments and actions of human beings, and leading to a series of counteractions which prove themselves to be significant. The only way to explain this world is to change it. Action must become the test of theory.

Selecting rather at random two sentences from Section Reports V and VI of the latest World Council Assembly, one discovers the absence of sufficient diagnosis and treatment of recurrent social ills. In the Report of Section V we read:

The structures of government on the national and local levels, within the religious communities, educational institutions and in employment, must become more responsive to the will of all the persons belonging to these various communities, and must provide for protection against manipulation by powerful interests.

Section VI offers the following insight:

Poverty, we are learning, is caused primarily by unjust structures that leave resources in the hands of a few within nations and among nations, and . . . therefore one of the main tasks of the Church when it expresses its solidarity with the poor is to oppose these structures at all levels. . . . The role of Christians and the Churches will be to assist in the definition, validation and articulation of just political, economic and social objectives and in translating them into action.[12]

One is inclined to ask immediately *how* exactly unjust structures came into being historically, *who* still empirically contributes to them, *who* still directly suffers from them, and *how* they can be systematically opposed, broken down, and changed into more just structures. One goes on to ask precisely *which* persons and *which* groups are in strategic revolutionary positions and have sufficient organized political power not only to prevent manipulation by the powerful but also to break their power. *Whom* exactly will the churches assist in the definition of new objectives? *Who* desires and requests their assistance? Are the churches not out of touch with historical reality when they wish to struggle *for* the poor but are unable to struggle *in the midst of and with* the poor? Do they really consider themselves a part of complex oppressive structures as they frequently accept the role of a chief apologist for or a passive spectator of an unjust social order? Is there not still far too little and precise information about their tacit adaptation to consolidating liberal, centrist, or socialist ideologies? For what precise reasons do Christians still object to the use of Marxist terms such as "proletariat," "class struggle," "ideology," "permanent revolution," "surplus value," "economic determinism," etc.? Are their terms really any better?

The current and most successful ecumenical action programs also have to be subjected to this long and painful interrogation. There is no doubt, of course, that the World Council of Churches' Programme to Combat Racism assists the churches to translate their long-term agreement on racial justice into effective programs through which victims of racism themselves may have a fuller share in power and so realize their own identity in society. Its Commission on the Churches' Participation in Development has made considerable progress in experimenting with partnership patterns in which the people of developing countries have the power to establish their own priorities and make their decisions. The Commission of the Churches on International Affairs advances at various times statements and proposals on such issues as disarmament, nuclear weapons testing, human rights, religious liberty, refugees, economic assistance, and national self-determination. The Council can hardly be accused of making irresponsible decisions and obstructing the cause of justice. Its actions originate from real compassion and deep solidarity with peoples in hardship, anxiety, and want.

Yet all these actions seem to validate the reluctance of Christian situation ethics to contribute *too directly* to the exposure of the primary causes of inequality, injustice, and collective egoism, not to participate *too directly* in the search for scientific economic planning (particularly in the poor countries), and not to stimulate *too directly* any radical change in suffocating and corrupt political structures.

Also the churches in their respective countries and their numerous organizations and agencies are very reluctant, if not entirely unwilling or unable, to unearth the roots of the relations and tendencies of traditional society, to mobilize the masses for active engagement in the shaping of a different society, and to interfere legally or illegally with government policies. Being opposed to all forms of popular struggle for liberation, the official churches and ruling political party (or parties), on the contrary, are all too often talking the same refined language of obedience and dependence; the institutional churches serve all too frequently as instruments of governments' ends. Even if a search for alternative social structures or a theology of (quasi) liberation is offered, the largest sector of populations in pressing need of true liberation does not know how to move forward. Again, one has to ask what it means that the churches have "to assist in the definition, validation and articulation of just political, economic and social objectives and translating them into action." *Who* actually does the competent defining and the accurate translating, *for whom* and *with whom* and *toward what end*?

Christian situation ethics reflects its limitations as it deems it rather unprofitable and superfluous to detect and to describe the ideological undercurrents and components of its own considerations. It also looks suspicious when we find it constantly worrying about the positive impact of its suggested activities on a greater manifestation of the oneness and wholeness of the church. That worry is more and more unfounded. It has become quite clear that, although some churches and individual Christians do not agree with certain "progressive" international actions, the world Christian fellowship as a whole is not threatened by strong opposition and deplorable division. The real crux of Christian situation ethics is whether the solidarity with peoples and nations it recommends is based on differentiation: that is, on the very existence of peoples and nations, not to be secretly absorbed into the churches themselves nor to be instrumentally used for their own self-realization and salvation. Solidarity is genuine and will lead to a greater humanization of societies only if the intricate inhuman structures of these societies are meticulously scrutinized, tackled, and altered by both insiders and outsiders of these societies deep below the surface, at the very depths. To this end an ideology welding the collective aspirations, energies, and commitments of peoples together is absolutely essential.

A Just, Participatory, and Sustainable Society

The World Council of Churches' Sub-unit on Church and Society, with the cooperation of the Commission on the Churches' Participation in Development and the Secretariat on Urban Industrial Missions organized at Bucharest, in 1974, a conference in order to conclude the five-year Council's Study Programme on the Future of Man and Society in a World of Science-Based Technology. During the discussions on the significance for the future of pressures of technology and population on environment and of natural limits to growth, self-reliance, and the technical options of developing countries, the quality of life and the human implications of further technological change, a "long-term concept of a sustainable and just society" was introduced. "In essence," the conference report concludes:

the sustainable society will be one with a stable population and with a fixed material wealth per person, a society actively pursuing quality of life in basically non-material dimensions such as leisure, service, arts, education, sports. In the sustainable state, problems will appear at a more manageable rate than today. People will be able to afford the luxury of delaying the use of new technology to increase human options (e.g. through an expansion of the global productivity or improved capacity to live a better life within existing limits) only after the unavoidable side effects are unearthed and publicized. More concretely, we foresee a world where (1) the security of the individual, (2) the redistribution of material wealth and (3) implementation of a maximum consumption level are effected by a transnational social security system dividing the responsibility for the fate of the individual among all people.

The Conference recommended that the World Council sponsor a study by its Sub-unit on Church and Society on the sustainable and just society, particularly in regard to policies for amelioration of adverse effects of the following issues on social justice, nationally and internationally:

(a) the impact on the less industrialized nations of a stabilization of the material activity of the industrialized world, (b) the effects on employment of stabilization of material production, (c) alternative development strategies for less industrialized countries, compatible with the ideal of a sustainable state, (d) patterns of optimum international division of labour and localization of production, resource consumption, and pollution, (e) the establishment of a global progressive income-tax levied and re-allocated by a transnational body to form the basis for a world that insures the security of the individual, (f) whether foreign capital and expertise, in as much as it is already present, can be utilized in a constructive way without the traditional elements of exploitation, (g) the bringing of defence, pollution control and resource rationing under control of a transnational body.[13]

The idea of a "sustainable and just society" was reintroduced into the World Council's Assembly at Nairobi. Participants in Section VI concentrated on the ethical problems in the transition to such a society. A "search for alternative development strategies for less industrialized countries, new patterns of optimal international division of labour, the use of foreign capital and expertise, international control of such matters as pollution and resource rationing" was suggested. The Report further added: "The basic goal remains: nobody should increase their affluence until everybody has their essentials."[14]

In conceiving the idea of a just, participatory, and sustainable society, the ecumenical movement has indulged, I am afraid, in a noble but also deceptive daydream. The nightmares of the world's Calcuttas are totally underestimated and disastrously ignored. One wonders how representatives of world Christianity found the time and the tranquillity to engage in such ambiguous and unrealistic thinking. Surely, grave problems such as the energy crisis, the squandering of natural resources, environmental deterioration, pollution, rising unemployment, urbanization, human settlements, and improving the quality of life preoccupy the technological and post-industrial western hemisphere. Scientists, engineers, economists, sociologists, and politicians are greatly pressed for transnational remedies and alternatives. But the Christian experts at Bucharest, speaking of "the swelling material activity on our fragile, finite planet," had clearly only the "developed" and "mature" western world in mind. It is only this part of the world that can afford the luxury of working for "a successful transition to a sustainable society."

But that eventual transition cannot take place except at the dire cost of Third World nations. It is a sheer illusion to expect that a consolidation of the maximum standards of living in the West will automatically result in a raising of the minimum standards of living in the East and the South. The United Nations World Food Conference in Rome and the World Population Conference in Bucharest reported four years ago that the situation we were often so confidently told could never happen is now likely to happen: worldwide famine that will kill millions of people and reduce even further the precarious standard of living of hundreds of millions of others. Even if the affluent societies were to succeed in implementing a transnational program, as outlined by the World Council of Churches' Conference at Bucharest, within their own provinces, their moral conscience will not be soothed by the misfortune of chronically underdeveloped nations.

When we analyze the engine of capitalist economic development in underdeveloped countries, at least five major faults can be found. These are the crisis in food production, the fast upward climb in migration, unemployment, and slum creation, together with an increasing maldistribution of income. The urban population of the Third World rose at an annual rate of 4 percent between 1920 and 1960, twice the rate in the developed countries during their time of development. A frighteningly high proportion of countryside migrants continues to end up in the towns without jobs, and often without a shelter.

Underemployment is even worse than unemployment. In a developed economy an expanding tertiary sector is a sign of progress. Services are the harvest of economic achievement. This is quite the reverse in Latin America, Africa, and Asia—services are parasitic, drawing odd coins from the pockets of wealthier passersby. The danger of Fourth World underemployment is that it is a disease that conventional economic growth cannot cure. It is too pathological, too far gone for the urban-industrial treatment to have any effect. In an attempt to show just how impossible the situation is, a recent Organization for Economic Co-operation and Development report has calculated that in order to eradicate within a decade the existing rural and urban underemployment, industrial production would have to increase by 30 to 35 percent a year. The report not surprisingly concludes:

Thus eradication of general under-employment through the development of industrial employment is a practical impossibility in the medium term.

All the evidence suggests that the escape route from poverty that leads through the city and the industrial sector is fraught with many more difficulties than was thought likely when newly independent countries started on this path a few decades ago. It is ironic indeed that both the major schools of economic thought—western capitalist and eastern European socialist—preached similar false solutions. Moscow-orientated socialists argued that real independence is impossible without a strong industrial base while capitalists were convinced that a developing industrial sector is the most effective way of attracting outside capital. The unproductive countries are now landed with the results of this mistaken advice—chronic food shortages, a demoralized countryside, a fast-expanding urban slum population, and a spectacular inequality between a few rich and millions of poor people.

Underdeveloped nations themselves share to a large extent the responsibility for inveterate underdevelopment. The absence of an appropriate and consistent agricultural policy is the root of their failure to raise even minimally the most primitive standards of living. Peasant farmers in many countries in Asia, Africa, and Latin America use the resources currently at their disposal inefficiently. A large stock of idle labor and land resources could be brought into production. Some obvious requisites for modernization are the change in repressive structures of land tenure; increased production through new forms of input, particularly improved seeds and fertilizers; provision for credit facilities; and educational institutions to teach farmers to use simple innovations. But instead of concentrating on the critical role of peasant agriculture in national development and directing policy attention to the analysis of the means of development of this large sector of the country's economy, modernization is sought in other sectors. Most of the scarce capital available is not invested in the existing stock of agricultural resources but in industrial production, which raises the economic level only of the small ruling class. Governments, moreover, do not succeed in discouraging and preventing the rural population from flocking into the cities where only more hunger and misery are awaiting them.

Among the few Third World nations that have consistently favored agricultural self-reliance and development, China should be mentioned. After decades of catastrophic droughts, harvest calamities, and massive starvation, its food production is now adequate, and though its population will increase to 1 billion Chinese in 1985, it is predicted that its agricultural product and industrial output will at least double, and possibly treble. A team of American agricultural specialists returning from a visit to China a few years ago stated:

China appears to have raised agricultural production and evened the distribution of food so successfully that it seems well protected against the food shortages now afflicting the underdeveloped world.[15]

China's approach to industry has been experimental and cautious, reflecting a deep reluctance to subvert agriculture as the base of its economy. Being instinctively apprehensive at the prospect of peasants moving in droves to the cities, the communists have called a halt to urbanization. Industry is cultivated in the countryside. People continue to live in the villages and to farm the land, while learning the techniques of industry in order to make their communes more productive. Hospitals, schools, administrators, and technicians are shifted from urban centers to the villages where they are needed. In the vast country with its huge population unemployment and underemployment do not exist. The Chinese people, formerly so fragmented, humiliated, exploited, and insecure, have been united in common goals of socialist nation building.

Christian social ethics, of course, subjects Maoism to a barrage of interrogations. Among the many questions, I list only the following: Was the acceptance of the Marxist-Leninist ideology and a thorough indigenization of communist principles in a Chinese context the only way out of a century-long submission and surrender to foreign powers? Do we really know what price in terms of human suffering and loss of individual freedom has been paid by the Chinese people for their economic and social success? Can Maoist claims be verified that individual persons can be changed and transformed into new human beings by consistently conditioning and controlling their behavior? Is not the China model an indigenous model, not designed for export to other cultures? As industrialization proceeds and the economy becomes more sophisticated, will the Maoists be able to solve those complicated problems which are burdening the advanced industrial nations? To what extent is the entire political system based on messianic nationalism, cultural aggressiveness, and Asian xenophobia? Still more questions can be raised and several pertinent answers have to be given.

But Maoists also interrogate Christians. Is it not deeply ironical, they can ask, that Christian social theology nowadays envisages "a society actively pursuing quality of life in basically non-material dimensions such as leisure, service, arts, education, sports," while Karl Marx already one hundred years ago had a dream that in the classless society humanity will hunt in the morning, fish in the afternoon, raise cattle in the evening, and discuss matters critically after supper, without ever becoming hunters, fishers, cattle raisers, or critics? Is not the fundamental difference between Christianity and Marxism-Leninism that Christianity, at least according to the Bucharest Christian World Conference report, holds that some "ideal" state will be reached as soon as a fixed material wealth per *person* is internationally agreed upon and the security of the individual will be guaranteed by a transnational social security system, while Marx predicted and Mao repeated that long and merciless struggles between *all* exploiters and *all* exploited and a long dictatorship of the proletariat are inevitable before humankind will regain its lost paradise? It is indeed deeply ironical that the Maoists have introduced the idea of perpetual cultural revolution which may last ten thousand years or more, while contemporary Christian ethics falls prey to a cheap realized eschatology. Ecumenical theology has overlooked, and this a serious omission, the fact that the realism of the cross of Jesus Christ and the realistic analysis of human history render any simple optimism and any easy short-term hopes about a sustainable and just society illusory and inhuman. There are no grounds for simplistic expectations either in the advance of justice in the world or in the churches as agents in relation to such advances.

Human beings are constantly inflicting suffering on other human beings and suffer at the hands of their fellow human beings. The structures and patterns of various societies perpetuate these sufferings and inhumanities, and those who enjoy privilege and power fight to keep it so.

The choice between Christian situation ethics or Maoist practice in Calcutta's society for that reason is not a difficult one, regardless of the fact that it is true that the "just, participatory and sustainable society" model is lifted up for sanctification by God, and the China model is stained by proud nationalism and maintained exclusively in the name of the people. Calcutta will never benefit from alternative development strategies for less industrialized countries, compatible with the ideal of a sustainable state. Its disease and hunger problems will not be solved when rich nations decide to reduce their conspicuous consumption. And its numerous square miles of slums will not be cleaned up when the traditional elements of exploitation are removed from foreign capital and expertise. What Calcutta needs is a strong socialist regime which brings strong ideological pressures to bear on the total population and unearths the rotten roots of its political and socio-economic infrastructure.

This, of course, does not ensure the security of each individual today or tomorrow. It will bring much limitation to individual freedom, more suffering, and much anxiety about each person's place in the newly to be constructed society. But the suffering and the anxieties cannot be so great and intense as they are today. And the shortcomings and injustices of the "leftist" regime tomorrow cannot exceed those of the "liberal" regime today. It will be possible to recapture a vision of the wholeness of the human being and an anticipation of a common system of beliefs leading toward a new communitarian ethics. Naturally, the search for radical solutions is never free from hasty judgments, false denunciations, and errors of economic analysis and social planning. But a socialist ideology gradually eliminating hunger, malnutrition, and want is more human than any Christian ideology offering only would-be solutions to the number one universal problem: extreme world poverty.

If only world Christianity would dare to say that in many countries of this world a more definite shape of society must indeed be ideologically defined, that all Christians in particular circumstances must earnestly examine their consciences as to whether they should not contribute to or even participate more actively in a long overdue revolution and stop glorifying precious democratic freedoms of the West, which cannot be traced back to and quoted from the New Testament; if only ecumenical conferences would discover that the solution of complicated theological problems (such as "clarifying the meaning of the Gospel in contexts where Christian faith and ideologies tend to be mixed up, leading to theological confusion and ethical impotence"[16]) does not take place in the realm of intellectual and uncommitted theological reflection, but in the actual context of daily ideological struggle and ideological dialogue directed and constantly corrected by the faith in Jesus Christ; if only Christians could properly deal with a subject like "ideology as a secular faith," not arguing that *they* have not fallen into the trap of ideology and that *they* have always recourse to transcendental wisdom, but frankly conceding that they too do not always use ideology exclusively as a tool for analyzing and understanding the social process: then ecumenical Christianity would gain greater relevance and credibility. It could not be accused of having included "ideologies" in the theme "Seeking Community—The Common Search of People of Various Faiths, Cultures and Ideologies," just to prove that it is open to secular social concerns and methods, while in fact it denies the legitimacy and achievements of Marxist regimes, on the ground that they lack any authentic religious reference, and gravely disregard the sacredness of personality essential to the Christian faith.

The ecumenical movement would be a wider movement of human liberation, not so preoccupied with and fascinated by its own impact and accomplishments, leaving room to ideological communities committed to a surrender of self on behalf of the community and to goals beyond self in tomorrow's history. It is not accidental that an American Christian, after returning from a visit to China, asked whether:

due to religious hypocrisy, it is not possible that God has become so disgusted with the "believers", that he has decided to turn the moral future of mankind over to "nonbelievers."[17]

Looking at Calcutta that question can be answered. God surely needs many socialists and communists to make the impact of his kingdom known to all those who hunger and thirst for righteousness. The hunger and thirst in Calcutta dare not be stilled by a handful of rice and a sip of milk, just to keep people alive for a few more years. And Christians dare not speak any more of enlarging the areas of freedom in Calcutta through gradual social reforms or accelerating the coming of a sustainable affluent society.

6

THE ANGUISH OF THE CROSS

The following pages will not be devoted to a particular theory of the atonement or an up-to-date theology of salvation. I have no desire to retrace centuries-old theological understandings and expositions of the evidence of atonement. According to the exemplarist theory (eleventh century) Christ suffered on the cross in order to give a supreme example and to convey the message of divine forgiveness. The juridical theory of atonement (twelfth century) argued that Christ's death on the cross was a ransom, not paid to the Devil but to God, whose pure majesty had been outraged by the sins of humanity, his creature. According to the classic or dramatic theory (revived in the Reformation period) Christ battled, on the contrary, with the Devil and defeated him once and for all. The sacrificial theory of atonement, based on the letter to the Hebrews, stressed that the Old Testament sin offering through animals became perfect in Jesus Christ as he offered himself most freely as a true human sacrifice in total obedience. The divine truth cannot lie in one or the other theory of atonement and not even in their sum. Whether salvation is primarily divine deliverance, divine judgment, or resurrection through divine intervention must remain an open question.

Readers of these pages are entitled to their own personal beliefs and their own points of view. Since one of the lietmotifs of this book is world Christianity vis-à-vis the suffering and salvation of the world's Calcuttas, I wish to single out one profound mystery: Christ's personal suffering and death. The death of Jesus on the cross, it is true, is seen by the Christian tradition not just as the execution of a person who proved inconvenient and dangerous to the authorities. The cross is a part of a divine drama that has cosmic significance. The historical event of the crucifixion is given depth through mythological and doctrinal dimensions. Nevertheless, I think it is quite possible and necessary to concentrate on Christ's agony on the cross and to let his words "My God, why hast thou forsaken me" speak for themselves, without developing a fully fledged doctrinal theory of atonement, reconciliation, and salvation.

Many theologies of the cross have served to cover up the lies and vanity, the lust for power, and the fearfulness of Christian churches. By propagating elaborate religious theories on God's way of dealing with humanity, Christianity has often become an alienated, divisive, and oppressive force in this world. On the following few pages we will see that the agony of the crucified Christ is a real challenge to Christian theology, Christian mission, and the Christian churches that dare to call themselves by his name. Whether world Christianity is ever afresh finding its unique identity and whether the ecumenical movement has a mission at all in Calcutta's society depends solely on the critical reality of the cross and a deep apprehension of the pain of the negative. Not metaphysical or theological speculation on the "why" and "wherefore" of God's decision to be reconciled with humanity through the cross of his Son, but the recognition of the very fact that God himself is capable of ineffable suffering can deliver the churches from their false identity and their irrelevant role in society. Sharing in the agony of Christ, contemporary Christendom will be led out of its difficulties whether in regard to the seeking of community with families of other faiths, to practicing critical solidarity with ideological movements and groups, to being true ambassadors for Christ to the world, or to tracing the ever widening frontiers of God's coming kingdom to one's neighbor, near or far away.

The classical symbol of the ecumenical movement has been a ship with a cross as the mast, set out on an unknown voyage. The General Secretary of the World Council of Churches noticed five years ago that, although the symbol has been modernized and the sea has been made more choppy, the ship has "remained solid, stately and smooth moving." He added:

We shall have to get our artist to re-design the ship so that it can be shown to be rolling uneasily over the waves in danger of being overwhelmed.[1]

The danger of being shipwrecked is indeed very real, and corresponds to Christ's desperate struggle on the cross. The cry "Our God, why hast thou forsaken us" is carried away by the roaring waves and the ocean winds.

Ecumenical official reports and statements, however, have very little to say about the hopeless suffering of Jesus Christ. The cross, in fact, has only been mentioned at rare intervals at assemblies and other major gatherings since 1948. Most references to the cross emphasize Christ's victory over death, the forgiveness and reconciliation by God, the creation of the new human being, or the freedom of discipleship leading to a new solidarity with all men and women. On a few occasions, a comment has been made on Christ's self-humiliation, but that self-humiliation is enshrined in glory and enables the church to witness to that glory and to manifest its faithful servanthood in the world.

Right from the beginning twentieth-century Christianity on the whole has been little astonished and appalled by the fact that Jesus Christ agonized and died a criminal's death on the cross. There is no awareness in depth that the foolishness of God proved to be wiser than the wisdom of human beings. The fact that the resurrected body of Christ bears the marks of his crucifixion and presumably so to all eternity seems to be forgotten. In the sentence: "I am the first and the last, and the living one; I *died*, and behold I am alive for evermore," only the word "alive" is underlined. But the heart of the Gospel is the cross of Jesus Christ revealing the utter pain and the utter love of God. It was the great merit of the Japanese theologian Kitamori to show that the pain of God belongs to his eternal being. "Why does Jesus' teaching seem to place the love of God above the pain of God when Jesus is the very pain of God?" he asks. "Every form of docetism results in a denial of the pain of God." In the thought of both Jesus and Paul, the pain of God and the love of God indissolubly unite to form a unity in the "love rooted in pain." The task of the "theology of the pain of God," according to Kitamori, is "to win over the theology which advocates a God who has no pain."[2]

That pain belongs to the eternal essence of God Dietrich Bonhoeffer also discovered more than thirty years ago when he wrote shortly before his execution:

God lets himself be pushed out of the world on the cross. He is weak and powerless in the world, and that is precisely the way, the only way, in which he is with us and helps us. Matthew 8:17 makes it quite clear that Christ helps us, not by virtue of his omnipotence, but by virtue of his weakness and suffering. . . . Only the suffering God can help. . . . That is a reversal of what the religious man expects from God. Man is summoned to share in God's suffering at the hands of a godless world.[3]

In one of his more recent books, *The Crucified God,* Jürgen Moltmann develops a theology of the suffering of God similar to that of Bonhoeffer and Kitamori. In the introduction he writes: "Either Jesus who was abandoned by God is the end of all theology or he is the beginning of a specifically Christian, and therefore critical and liberating, theology and life." In the chapter entitled "The Resistance of the Cross against Its Interpretations," Moltmann makes it clear that radical Christian faith committing itself without reserve to the crucified God is hazardous. This faith

does not promise the confirmation of one's own conceptions, hopes and good intentions. It promises first of all pain of repentance and fundamental change. It offers no recipe for success. It does not create a home for man and integrate him in society, but makes him "homeless" and "rootless," and liberates him in following Christ who was homeless and rootless.

In the next paragraph he continues:

The symbol of the cross in the church points to the God who was crucified not between two candles on an altar, but between two thieves in the place of the skull, where the outcasts belong, outside the gates of the city. It does not invite thought but a change of mind. It is a symbol which therefore leads out of the church and out of religious longing into the fellowship of the oppressed and abandoned. On the other hand, it is a symbol which calls the oppressed and the godless into the church and through the church into the fellowship of the crucified God. Where this contradiction in the cross, and its revolution in religious values, is forgotten, the cross ceases to be a symbol and becomes an idol, and no longer invites a revolution in thought, but the end of thought in self-affirmation.[4]

The Anguish of False Identity

These few paragraphs on Christ's agony on the cross and the sharing of humanity in the fellowship of the crucified God perhaps enable us now to indicate more concretely in which directions Christianity can move beyond its present solitude and stagnation. As the crucial issue of the specific identity of the church and the identity of each individual—the two never exist apart and cannot be separated—is before us, it should be perfectly clear that all existence in faith is conditioned by a twofold truth. Where there is no certainty and lucidity about Christian identity, no authentic contribution can be made to the universal search and struggle for a truly human identity. But where Christian identity is maintained and proclaimed apart from the universal search and struggle for a truly human identity, the very basis and contents of the specific identity, namely, the cross of Jesus Christ "ceases to be a symbol and becomes an idol."

It is the suffering and agony of Christ on the cross which holds the Christian and the human identity together. When the church and its believers do not experience that "God lets himself be pushed out of the world on the cross" and they wish to be powerful, respectable, and effective in the world, their actions aiming at the enhancement of human dignity and the strengthening of human identity are tinged by a false Christian identity. On the other hand, when the church and its faithful claim that they are affected by the conflicts, struggles, and distresses of this world and share in humanity's calamities and sufferings, but do not experience the endless pain of the incarnate Son of God, their perhaps noble human identity can only be falsely derived from their specific Christian identity. The ethic of pain which implies becoming "homeless and rootless" can be realized only through the pain of God who became "homeless and rootless" in Jesus Christ. Christians can feel their neighbors' pains as intensively as their own, not because they are joined together in the same fate, but because they are all embraced in the same suffering of God.

When Christianity changes the crucified Christ into a victorious Christ and proclaims God's reconciliation with humanity in triumphalistic terms, it suffers from a false identity. Unless all churches and Christians share in the agony of Christ and practice repentance, there can be no authentic worldwide awareness of the universal glory of God. As long as it is taken for granted that Christian organizations stand at the frontiers of the progressive history of salvation and need not worry about a false Christian identity, the Gospel is announced in dehumanizing ways and all sorts of programs are carried out, not in response to the anguish and groans of humanity but in the name of their obvious national and international validity. As Christ is agonizing in the midst of the troubled world —he is crucified "not on the altar between two candles, but outside the city between two thieves"—his universal church must deeply share in his sufferings in the world if it is to relieve some of the burdens of downtrodden and desolate peoples. The strategies of Christian programs cannot be discussed under the altar candlelight, nor are they theologically to be justified in animated ecclesiastical conferences. They arise automatically and authentically out of human confusions, weaknesses, and struggles in which Christ himself is caught. Their relevance depends simultaneously on the insight, implications, and participation in the suffering of Christ and the sufferings of his fellow human beings. This is also true for an international Christian organization like the World Council of Churches.

"Thus programmes in their humanization aspect," Canon David Jenkins, former Director of the World Council's Humanum Studies, writes:

require to be handled with great care and discernment. Megalomania needs to be avoided. It is not the role of the World Council of Churches, nor of the churches, to be agents in the world of the whole work of God and all the good work of men. They are to respond to the work of God and to contribute to the work of men. Programmes therefore must be planned as limited means of carrying out roles that are enabling, initiating or entrepreneurial. Time and resources must be allowed for gaining awareness of what is being done in the world or the churches at large and it must never be supposed that a World Council programme can justify the status of a truly representative programme. All programmes are "on behalf of", "in response to" and "in order to promote." They must not be given ontological or permanent status. . . .[5]

These insights and concerns are not yet sufficiently and widely shared in the churches or in the ecumenical movement. On the contrary, not long ago many Christian communities were bogged down in the discussion of a theological problem of a very different nature. Voices in Eastern Orthodox circles and in various evangelical groups stated that "genuine Christian ecumenism," which is supposed to enhance the unity of the church, has been supplanted by "secular ecumenism." The ecumenical movement, they argued, is plunged into a crisis, because it is far too much "horizontally" orientated. True salvation must be understood in "vertical" terms. The search for salvation has to continue within the fellowship of all believers and cannot be connected with the church's involvement in the world. Repentance and renewal take place in the confrontation with God in Jesus Christ, and not on a socio-political level of life. Christian identity is given in the eucharistic communion and not in manifestations of understanding and solidarity with people adhering to different faiths or purely ideological convictions. As soon as the church participates directly in the political and socio-economic battles of this world it only "copies human absolute ideologies," they maintained, and fails to proclaim the Gospel.

This passionate discussion on the horizontal and vertical orientation of the ecumenical movement circled around an isolated and in the end a false problem, because the churches did not seem disturbed by the danger of acquiring both a false Christian identity and a false human identity. As there was not sufficient surprise and gratefulness that the agonizing Christ "leads the church out of its religious longing into the fellowship of the abandoned and oppressed," the question of "combining harmoniously the vertical and horizontal dimensions of activities" was artificially fabricated in order to cover up the false identities and to underline the relevance of the ecumenical movement in the modern world. Both "verticalists" and "horizontalists" had a real concern as long as they completed and sustained each other. Both, however, were on a false track when they were suspicious of each other and tried to correct the other's position as they did not wholly identify themselves with the Christ who suffered and died for the entire world. It was a "static" and therefore a false truth that true Christian identity is provided for in the one catholic church and the eucharistic fellow-

ship, even if the manifestation of the one universal church and the
Lord's Supper are considered as starting points for all the churches'
social actions. The desire for "ecclesiastical" and ecclesiastically
conditioned ecumenical identity—whether vertically or horizontally
motivated—leads quickly to an anxious Christian self-assertion and
to a Christian depreciation of the world as a mere field of action.
True Christian identity is always new and in "dynamic" ways given to
all who respond to "God's summons to share in his suffering at the
hands of a godless world."

The "horizontal-vertical" tension, rather unexpectedly, was not
mentioned at all at the Fifth Assembly of the World Council of
Churches. On the contrary, to the astonishment of a great number of
participants, many assembly sessions refused to separate faith from
social action, and witness to Christ from political involvement. The
call for a spirituality, a style of life for more effective evangelism, and
the call to accept the challenges of burning world issues went hand in
hand. Significantly, even the most contested World Council activity
—the Programme to Combat Racism—was not repudiated. The
identification with the poor and the oppressed, it was emphasized
more strongly than before, is closely related to the expression of new
and authentic styles of Christian living. This is no doubt a step in a
promising new direction. The only problem is how the dialectic
between faith and action, confession and commitment can be lived
out in various concrete situations. If the agonizing Christ has not an
immediate bearing both on social (ideological) action and the
spiritual shape of the Christian community, the faith-and-deed
dialectic remains as much imperfect as the "horizontal-vertical"
deadlock is sterile.

The Anguish of Mission

"Only the suffering God can help. . . .That is a reversal of what the
religious man expects from God." This sentence provides a proper
setting for Christian missions. Since Christianity can never claim to
understand Christ's agony on the cross in its greatest depth and must
admit that it is indeed very difficult, if not impossible, to believe in
the effective help of a suffering God, it needs to share honestly and
openly the resistance of all religions to the idea of divine vicarious

suffering. Not surprisingly the vast majority of Christians are totally ignorant of the various violent and horrified reactions against the biblical accounts of the crucifixion of the incarnate Son of God. The church confidently believes that a closer examination of Christ's death and Resurrection will eventually ease the anger and disgust of religious and unreligious men and women. The crucifixion resulted after all in a great victory and not in a tragic defeat. The cross has to be interpreted as the means of the creation of a common brotherhood for the divided and alienated human race.

However world Christianity may argue today, it still conveniently overlooks the fact that the cross has been widely rejected for two millennia on the ground that it contradicts all human conceptions of beauty, righteousness, and the moral integrity of humanity. Faith in the crucified God cannot be generously recommended as a noble and good faith, since God approached as the supreme Being and the supreme Good corresponds far more to the religious longing for fellowship with the Creator and Sustainer of the universe. For that reason it will be a profitable exercise to look at the negative interpretations of the cross and the narratives of Christ's crucifixion.

In the Roman empire crucifixion was considered so shameful a penalty that it was reserved for slaves and criminals of the lowest class. Execution on a cross could not be inflicted on Roman citizens. Consequently, according to Greek and Roman humanism, nothing was more vulgar and godless than the veneration of the crucified Christ. Christians were persecuted as incorrigible blasphemers and atheists. In Israelite understanding death by crucifixion brought Jesus into public disrepute. It placed him under an ancient curse, ". . . for it is written: Cursed be every one who hangs on a tree" (Gal. 3:13; cf. Deut. 21:23). Nothing in the Old Testament or in Jewish lore had prepared the Jew for the thought that the Messiah should be thus handled. The cross has remained the greatest obstacle in all efforts to convert Jews to the new faith. Precisely the claim that in Jesus the Word of God has come in the flesh is in Jewish eyes the absolute scandalousness of the Gospel. A condemned blasphemer risen from the dead cannot be categorized otherwise than being in revolt against the righteousness of God revealed in the Mosaic law. A cross is the "fitting close of such a life of rejection, scorn and defeat."

Even less is Christianity aware of the natural dislike of and the strong objections to the "theology of the pain of God" in Muslim, Buddhist, and Hindu faiths. To Muslims it is extremely difficult to understand that the Father would allow his beloved Son to die on the cross without causing a convulsion of nature. Since God always protects his faithful servants and is never defeated it follows that those who thought that Jesus was crucified must have been mistaken. It is possible that Jesus in the garden of Gethsemane opted for the way of the cross—Muhammad opted for the way of cooperating with the power of God, and becoming God's agent in the elimination of evil and injustice—but after Gethsemane "the role of history ends and the role of credal faith begins." The stories relating to the crucifixion and the Resurrection of Jesus are poetical and imaginary and cannot be valued as historical accounts.

To rationalistic Muslim belief there is no doubt that the "Jewish Messiah" was saved at the last moment by divine agency from an ignominious death. The Prophet escaped to the regions of the East, where safe from Jewish persecution he peacefully pursued his mission, and eventually died. Not only the mythical story of crucifixion but the Christian doctrines of original sin, atonement, and justification by faith are, according to Muslim traditions, disastrous to human morality. Islam repudiates the Christian teaching of hereditary depravity and "natural sinfulness," rejects the idea that an angry God can be appeased only by the sacrifice of a particularly precious human being as a primitive conception of antiquity, and preaches forcefully the practice of peace, humility, charity, good works, the denial of self, and submission to God's will. Jesus, Muhammad himself was convinced, never wished his followers to understand his death as a sacrificial offering for the sins of humanity in general or their sins in particular. The Christian dogma of the Sonship of Jesus—the only begotten Son of God—is to be blamed for laying the basis of an immoral belief in the saving function of the cross. Islam has long considered itself as the true representative of Christianity revering the Prophet of Nazareth as one of the greatest moral teachers of the world who appeals to the heart and the intelligence of the natural human being.

Buddhism opposes just as strongly as Islam any idea of vicarious suffering and death. The crucified Christ is a terrible sight to any

Buddhist. Followers of Buddha assure us that they cannot help associating the crucifixion with "the sadistic impulse of a physically affected brain." Also the symbolism of eating Christ's body and drinking his blood is resented as utterly repulsive and distasteful. To think that a self exists is the start of all errors and evils, Buddhism asserts. As there is no self, no crucifixion is required, no sadism need be practiced, and no shocking sight need be displayed. The nonexisting ego need not be crucified. What man lacks, according to Buddha, is enlightenment which will dispel the cloud of ignorance and bring true peace and absolute freedom to humanity. Crucifixion is meaningless when not followed by resurrection. But in the resurrected Christ there is still "the odor of the body." In enlightenment, on the contrary, there is a total sense of transcendence "transforming the earth itself into the pure land." In contrast to Christ's death on a vertically erected cross, which suggests agitation, struggle, and exclusive self-sacrifice, Buddha dies peacefully, nonviolently, tolerantly, and rationally in a horizontal posture on a bed, surrounded by his disciples and many kinds of animals mourning his death.

As long as Christianity teaches that the self must be crucified, the fighting and overpowering of the self will end in a nightmare and produce only a misleading hope. The vertical position does not lead to salvation. The Nirvana-Buddha, on the contrary, can serenely assume a sitting or lying posture, because he has liberated himself from the enslavement of his nonexistent and only apparent empirical ego. It is a Christian delusion that the cross and the resurrection have changed the empirical self into a transcendental self. Human beings will reach paradise (the total liberation of themselves) only after their long cycle of rebirth comes to an end. The Buddha is the Way (*Magga*) and the Truth (*Bodhi*) on that long road.

The genius of Hinduism is its ability to absorb, to comprehend, and to offer a unique synthesis of various world religions. The Incarnation of Jesus Christ and his suffering and death pose no problem to the Hindu faith, for numerous divine incarnations (*Avataras*) in the course of world history are acknowledged. These divine manifestations are filled with the power of grace and never frustrated when immediate goals are not attained. Incarnations understand human nature and realize that time is needed for the world to assimilate their message. Also Jesus was never disappointed at the ignorance and weaknesses of human beings. He forgave those who crucified him, saying: "Father, forgive them, for they know not what they do." He fulfilled his purpose when he inspired a few persons with God-consciousness, who for their part transmitted his message through successive links of teachers and disciples. Christ's crucifixion and Resurrection are to Hindus not a scandal and an offense. The only real heresy of Christianity, in their eyes, is its claim to exclusive truth. Hinduism will never participate in the quarrel of the absolute validity of one religion over against another. Many divine names can be adored. They are all eminent clues to the transcendent, immortal, unembodied Brahma. Contemplating, lauding, and finally denying these names, humanity rises ever higher in these worlds until it will attain to the "Unity of the Person."

This summary of negative reactions to the narratives of Jesus' suffering on the cross and of grave objections to the theologies of the crucified God provides the background and environment for Christian mission and evangelism. It should be even more clear now that the transmission and the eventual acceptance of the New Testament message depends on the genuineness of the Christian identity, the trustworthy formulation of the "good news," and the authenticity of Christian social programs. Each of these three conditions is fulfilled only when the churches and their faithful are continuously absorbed and marked by God's immeasurable pain expressed in the agony of Jesus Christ. When Christianity states bluntly that the cross is the pivotal point of history from which all history, prior and subsequent, derives its meaning, Jews, Hindus, Buddhists, and Muslims have every right to doubt the genuineness of Christian identity, which expresses itself in such presumptuous words. Although it is true that the crucified Christ can bring the freedom which changes the world, the cross cannot be appreciated and loved at all as it always calls both the identity of the church and of the world into question. If the Christian message is not impregnated by the anguished cry "why hast thou forsaken us," Christians will not manage "to win over the theology which advocates a God who has no pain."

Taking the cross seriously requires an understanding of God as the passionate One who suffers in solidarity with suffering men and women in history. When the churches, which are committed to practice this faith, wish to promote justice and peace and to advance the quality of life and dignity of humanity, their admonishments and appeals will have a pioneering or prophetic character—to use rather daring adjectives—only if people of other faiths can discover that the churches themselves often go through inner crises because they have domesticated the crucified Christ in an all-round dogmatics of salvation and incorporated him in a neatly defined Christian community. An impassible and unchangeable church to which the Lord Jesus Christ himself is a stranger cannot speak to the heart of those who deeply believe that God is impassible and unchangeable. Such a church provides in fact all the arguments for not trusting and following the Son of God who represents his Father in anguish and pain.

Whether Buddhist or Hindu, Jew or Muslim, all are understandably on their guard when world Christianity preaches the social doctrine of a just, participatory, and sustainable society which will also provide bread and happiness to underdeveloped peoples. They cannot comprehend that the feverish pursuit of wealth, the devotion to luxury, and the chastened but still unfaltering belief in progress are derived from a Gospel of suffering and humility. The inability to endure pain and to relieve the poignant distress at home seems in their eyes to be diverted to the making of distant and doubtful converts among other religious communities. Thus Muslims cling even closer to their God who requires self-denial, meekness, charity, and total submission to his will. Buddhists will emphasize even more that the root of all evil and falsehood is the craving of humanity's precious imaginary ego and that humanity can be healed by following Buddha's path of rational, impassible, and serene enlightenment. And Hindus will protest even more strongly against Christianity's claim of absolute truth, as the church's superior and intolerant attitude toward other religions is incongruous with the love of God leading human beings through many divine incarnations to the liberating truth of the union of *Brahman* and *atman*.

The Anguish of Christian Presence in Calcutta

The perpetual struggle against a false Christian identity, a deficient Christian theology, and a dubious Christian service to neighbors reaches its greatest intensity in Calcutta. But precisely in Calcutta this threefold battle is not hopeless if it is fought in the name of and in the presence of the agonizing Christ. The environment of his crucifixion has not changed. There is no difference between the place of the skull and a Calcutta sidewalk. He is crucified in the midst of the lowest social class. Both the realism of the cross and the realism of human oppression and struggles cannot be more deeply expressed than on and around Calcutta's Howrah Bridge. The more Christians live face to face with the hopeless plight of the outcasts, who outnumber the privileged of sustainable societies, the more they share in Christ's agony and the more they discover the pain of the love of God.

Struggling against "man's inhumanity to man," there is no need to worry about a stable and recognizable identity, since participating in the suffering Christ will provide all the identity human beings require. There is no sense in building another Truth Lutheran Church or a Sacred Heart Roman Catholic Cathedral in Calcutta and inviting street dwellers to join the company of well-fed and steadfast believers. Such an invitation renders the discovery of God's unfathomable love more difficult. And no official theological vindication is required of church aid programs relieving the poverty, the hunger, and the aimlessness of many "underprivileged" people. Acts of charity and manifestations of solidarity will speak for themselves. If there is any theology of service and charity to be developed, it cannot but arise out of the daily struggles against the atrocities and injustices humans inflict upon other humans.

Not being trapped in the dehumanizing possibilities of announcing a misleading Gospel, of pretending a strong identity, and of fighting for the humanization of society for one's own preservation, Christians can practice a genuine and real presence in the Calcuttas of this world. As they know that God is in the midst of the exploited, the forgotten, and the downtrodden as the crucified one, who is the sign of hope because he is the embodiment of anguish, they will resist the temptation of organizing spectacular rallies for Christ and of absolutizing or idolizing any plan of rescue, assistance, and aid. As I pointed out in Chapter 3, a common search for community is possible only when the ultimate hopes of world religions are humanely lived out and profoundly tested against each other; costly chances of meeting fellow human beings as they are will not then be missed. Such encounters can still turn into an intellectual and obstinate comparing of various religious concepts, dogmas, and precepts without bringing the interlocutors closer together, except for some polite mutual assurance of common concerns and goals.

But Christians will ask again and again the question of the bearing of their faith—if that faith is to have any significance it must be something very simple—on daily life and death in Calcutta. They themselves will make great efforts to relinquish a coherent and all-enfolding exposition of their faith and to witness to their crucified God in sober and humble words. Everything pivots on the others' discovery of their human identity, which is truly human because it is permeated with the identity of the suffering Christ. All the beliefs that God is exclusively the All-good and the All-wise, that he is utterly aloof of evil and misery, and that humanity can overcome its tragic ignorance by eliminating its yearning for existence, will equally have to come to terms with the inhuman, chaotic, and revolting society of Calcutta. And these beliefs will be measured to an equal degree by the depth of the human identity imbued by the trust in a lofty but merciful God. Here the delicate task of Christian mission starts pointing to the true humanity of men and women in Christ and to the love of the creative, judging, and redeeming God. Instead of indulging in fantasies of successful conversion, Christians will continue to examine the intensity of their identification with the victorious, suffering Lord in order not to communicate again *their* understanding of the Gospel which will only diminish the human receptiveness for a truly liberating faith.

Christian presence will further imply a realistic and hopeful serving of men and women. No one pattern of showing human solidarity, of struggling for freedom, and of sharing love, can be set. The only criterion for help and the common pursuit of objectives is that western white Christianity—and all nonwhite Christians who are still being impressed by Atlantic wealth, ingenuity, and efficiency —should no longer attempt to preside over development projects, carried out in the name of the self-reliance and the dignity of indigenous peoples. I have already referred to the very real danger that national and international relief organizations and ecumenical agencies for development are run by activist Christians who have become experts in alleviating the burdens of evil, want, and distress of those who are silently classified as unfortunate, clumsy, uneducated, and indolent. Muslims, Hindus, and Buddhists are very sensitive to organized Christian religions determining the earthly standards of life and insinuating that these standards condition human well-being. Either the Gospel Christians preach is betrayed by their haughty attitude and their incessant meddling with other people's business or their ethical value standards are based on false claims of biblical revelation and truth, they reason. The Christian churches are indeed challenged by the individual and collective behavior of religious groups which make no distinction between spiritual devotion and material caring for others. The question must constantly be asked "Who is serving whom and how are others being served?"

Christian presence is finally open to the work of God through many human endeavors to work for a better society. As all charitable actions and development projects put together do not feed the majority of the hungry or clothe the majority of the naked, effective means for achieving the well-being of the majorities must be sought. Frequently only a revolution is the means of obtaining a government that will feed the hungry, clothe the naked, teach the uneducated, and perform works of charity. World Christianity should speak more openly and more frequently about the *human* possibilities and responsibilities of carrying out these tasks. It should rejoice publicly when people are clothed, housed, fed, and can lead dignified and meaningful lives. Christian publications in many languages speak too exclusively of the *churches'* resources and *their* responsibilities for contributing to a greater humanization of societies, as if God is not at work in humanity's struggles against exploitation, oppression, and injustice and as if these struggles are not responses to the divine command to love one's neighbor as oneself. Still worse, many attempts to change the infrastructure of a society are immediately interpreted "in the light of" a Christian theology of liberation or development, as if the churches have always sufficient wisdom and an absolute right to question the social achievement of any government or political movement whatever.

True Christian presence is open-eared and open-eyed everywhere but particularly in the utterly poor societies of this world. There is not much ground for boasting about the success of mission, achievements in the field of aid and development, and valuable advice to state and city authorities. We have seen in the preceding chapter that much socio-economic counsel given by a host of western experts to developing countries has had disastrous effects on both urban conglomerations and vast rural areas. In many Fourth World regions its seems almost impossible to correct and to reverse what with the help of affluent nations—and with the moral support of western churches—has been started as a promising industrial enterprise. When it comes to participating actively in national programs of self-reliance, socialization of property, state-controlled economic planning, socialized education and medicine, and the edification of a common ethos, Christians again have no reason to be proud of their record as innovators and promoters. In most socialist countries the churches play at the most a role of endorsing tacitly a given national ideology in order to safeguard their traditional institutional existence. Their approval of "progressive" Christian action programs on a worldwide scale enhances their image of not trailing too far behind far-reaching governmental policies and practices.

Naturally, Christians identifying themselves with their Lord Jesus Christ cannot but be reserved and critical of all human attempts to approximate a just and human society. Their God was crucified precisely because all men and women are sinners—that is, human beings not motivated only by purely altruistic instincts when they construct together a human community. "Serving the people" is only possible within the limits of human capacity and interest for living together according to common standards of values and ideals. Human beings are not capable as Jesus Christ was of suffering for humanity, of struggling with death in order that others may live, and of restoring the deepest human relationship among fellow human beings. In the shadow of the cross men and women continue to combat domination, exploitation, greed, and selfishness and share beyond their expectation in the promise that all partly achieved community among human beings will ultimately be liberated and fulfilled. In the same shadow of the cross Christianity must far more openly express its anguish of being truly present in this tumultuous and transient world. Its cries and groans have to be uttered in order that other believers and "nonbelievers" may discover for themselves how provisional and inadequate Christian relief programs are in comparison to the sufferings and torments of the church's Lord. Its cries and groans have to be heard in order that "non-Christians" and

Christians alike take their common task of changing the class-ridden structures of the old society and of shaping an ideological prototype of a new society still more seriously.

Its cries and groans must be voiced even more loudly in Calcutta so that slum dwellers, struck down by hunger, misery, and disease, do not die today or tomorrow without a glimpse of the one God in pain for their salvation. Christianity, in anguish of its identity, its mission, and its presence in the world, will be able to invite others "into the fellowship of the crucified God." The power of the suffering Christ is incomparably greater than the power of an omnipotent but fathomless God and the power of humanity to negate and to annihilate itself. The power of the militant and subversive Christ, inspiring Spartacus, Thomas Münzer, and Karl Marx to change radically the social structures of the world, is still incomparably greater than all communists in their deepest aspirations have been dreaming of. And the power of the crucified Christ is the only power in Calcutta because it has abolished death on the cross—the horrible death that so many of its citizens die daily.

7

SALVATION HISTORY

Discussing contemporary issues of inter-religious dialogue in various parts of the world, the common search for a world community of communities, and a critical solidarity with more radical ideological movements—in particular with the practice of Marxist ideology in China—we have seen that world Christianity has barely started to venture into these new directions of anticipations and concerns. We have also noticed that the very serious plight of Calcutta is intimately related to crucial questions of inter-religious dialogue, the place of Two-Thirds World nations in the emerging world community, and the application of suitable socialist systems to poor and overpopulated societies. In this chapter, in which again Calcutta and China will be criteria for the relevance of world Christianity, I wish to concentrate briefly on traditional theological understandings of world history and present approaches to the history of salvation in a truly universal context. It is in this connection that the worldwide relevance and trustworthiness of the Christian religion has even more closely to be examined.

There is still a great reluctance in Christianity to include "non-Christians" around the world and from beginning to end in God's design of salvation. This is due to various current interpretations of "salvation history"—the term is a literal translation of *Heilsgeschichte,* a concept developed by German theologians during the nineteenth century. According to certain theological schools "salvation history" is understood as a series of events of sacred history, including incarnation, redemption, and eschatology, taking place in a suprahistorical sphere and accessible only to faith, which is based exclusively on God's revelation of his way of dealing with humanity. Other theological views hold that the history of revelation and salvation advances through concrete events in actual history, of which Jesus Christ is the center and the culmination. The limitation of both theologies of salvation history is that only Christians can discern God's intention and purpose with humanity by accepting Christ as their Lord and Savior. Whether stress is laid upon God's unique revelation in Jesus Christ or upon God's saving acts in history—the story of the exodus and the deliverance of Israel is of primordial importance—it is only faith in Christ which makes sense of the witness of the biblical records. Where there is no faith in the saving Lord neither is there knowledge of the redeeming love of God nor discernment of God's wrestling with human history. The church, which was founded by Christ himself, is the storehouse of every necessary insight into God's plan of salvation and is called to proclaim his mighty acts of love to the ends of the earth.

Incomplete Theologies of History

The trouble with these theologies of salvation history is not only that they provide no room for nations and peoples of extrabiblical traditions but that they are deeply embedded in the Greco-Latin western culture. The concept of *oikoumene,* as I indicated in Chapter 2, served to distinguish carefully between the inhabited and the uninhabited earth. During the long Constantinian period the church in the West was proclaimed as the sign and seal of God's salvation. Outside the confines of the western Christian world, the mystery of salvation could not be comprehended unless the mission of the church in the name of Jesus Christ was dutifully accepted. Only quite recently has it been admitted in the theological debate that in announcing salvation the church has often limited itself to a mere restatement of the biblical witness. As salvation in the Bible presents itself as an ongoing event, a history in which God moves to achieve his purpose for humanity and the world, the church must identify and interpret this ongoing history. Its liberation theologies of the last decade have stressed that salvation is intimately related to the liberation struggles in a political, economic, or cultural context. The story of the Old Testament, Christianity stresses anew, is, after all, itself a dramatic story of a people's liberation.

Yet Christian theology interpreting the word of God in contemporary history does not seem to break out of the western historical and cultural framework. The so-called non-Christian peoples and nations still hardly come within the purview of theology proper. This is particularly evident when questions about the theological meaning of, for example, the new China are raised. Is there, in fact, some connection between the dramatic change in China and the salvific action of God in the world? Does the new China present a challenge to the Gospel of salvation interpreted and propagated by a church which is only seemingly universal? Needless to say, the achievements of China should in no way be exaggerated or romanticized. The real meaning of the Chinese revolutionary experience must be soberly evaluated. Our images of China must be tested against its constantly changing reality. China is not the paradigm of the kingdom of God and never will be. What we see happening in contemporary China seems, nevertheless, to be God's intensive wrestling with a people, perhaps in one way or another revealing and fulfilling still further his saving purpose. Out of the depth of their sufferings the Chinese have emerged with a new hope for the future. Not only is China a visible proof that a populous nation can survive at a simple but adequate standard of living, with fair distribution for all, but the social and political transformations brought about in the new China have unified and consolidated a quarter of the world's population into a form of society and lifestyle which are recapturing the vision of the wholeness of humanity and the wholeness of community.

Christian theology, however, still worries a great deal (and rightly) that God's saving acts, which are demonstrated in the Old and New Testament and also in the history of the church, should be arbitrarily multiplied in ongoing world history by sheer human reasoning. Although it is true that God's grace has been at work at all times in human history, not one historical event—other than the Christ-event—can be singled out as a determinative intervention of God in human affairs. The Incarnation of God in Jesus Christ is and always will be absolutely unique and determinative. It is dangerous to argue from God's alliance with Noah that China does not fall outside God's plan of salvation. It is equally risky to compare Mao Tse-tung with Cyrus, the Persian king of whom Daniel 9:26 speaks as God's anointed one. The parallel between the exodus of Moses and the

Long March should not be pressed too hard. Christians just like non-Christians are prone to confuse the historical with the ultimate, the achievement with the task that has not yet been performed. The apprehension of the revelation of God can always become a human idol. Mortal human beings should beware of establishing direct relationship between God's acts and historical events. It seems therefore much safer to renounce any theological attempt at interpreting the meaning of complex international politics in the light of "salvation history."

But the question recurs whether China since 1949 must fall outside the scope of a West-centered Judeo-Christian understanding of universal history. Much current Christian literature suggests that the era of the communist regime has to be considered as an interim period. The Maoists will slowly forget the long humiliating treatment of the West. All ideological fanaticism will run out after a while and the communist occupation of China can already be seen today as a providential preparation for the Christian message. This whole argumentation assumes that God is temporarily absent from China and will be present again when the banner of the Gospel is carried back some day from the West. This, of course, cannot be true. The new China as well as other nations are not to be treated anymore as objects of religious conversion. A British theologian writing recently on China came to the following conclusion:

The objection to a Communist regime most commonly voiced in this country is that it is totalitarian and coercive, whereas we are free. Though our freedoms are less absolute than they are imagined to be, the contrast can be granted.[1]

This assertion confirms that the *oikoumene* is in need of a new set of biblical and theological assumptions providing fresh insights into the acts of God in the "uninhabited world."

It is not my intention to develop here, even in outline, a more inclusive biblical theory of salvation history. No eminent theologian, as I said before, has so far been able to lead the Christian understanding of the history of redemption out of the past and present impasse. A few indications can be offered, however, of how Christian universalism may be conceived of biblically in terms of the *whole* world and *all* nations.

A Reassessment of Biblical Teachings

Pondering over the Old Testament understanding of world history, Christians have far too often overlooked the fact that the election of Abraham, and through him Israel, has as its setting the universal election of all people through Noah. God's covenant with Noah is a covenant with all humankind. In this covenant God not only promises never again to destroy the world in judgment, but to provide for the preservation of humanity in the matter of food, warmth, and bodily needs. He also gives dominion over creation to humankind as his underlord and sets up the order of society and government, without which human life could not survive. The covenant in Noah is not conditional upon the response of men and women to it; it is made on the initiative of God and is sustained by his faithfulness, despite human sin.

The other three special covenants, the covenant with Abraham (Gen. 17), the covenant with Israel at Horeb-Sinai (Exod. 19), and the new covenant in Jesus Christ (Matt. 26:28; 1 Cor. 11:25) do not abolish the first covenant. These covenants cannot become means for securing the particularity of certain limited communities. They are principally means for expressing the universality of God's sovereignty. When Israel boasts of its special relationship to God, the prophet Amos reminds the Israelites that God cares as much for the Ethiopians as for the people of Israel (Amos 9:7). According to Isaiah 40:2, God's chosen people is not free of judgment while other peoples receive judgement. On the contrary, it receives "at the Lord's hand double measure for all her sins." The prophet Ezekiel chides his people with the fact that it has more wickedly rebelled against God's laws and statutes than other nations and countries (Ezek. 5:6). Jeremiah prophesies that the Law of God will be within all people. Religious instruction and cultus will become unnecessary (Jer. 31:34). In this sense the covenant with Noah, which assures us that no human being is cut off from the knowledge of God save by his own depravity and that no human being is beyond the care and loving-kindness of God despite his depravity, will find its eschatological fulfillment.

Just as the covenant of disclosure formed through Abraham did not replace the earlier covenant in Noah, so too the church could not replace Israel in the covenant of disclosure. But as I just remarked, the church very soon did set outer limits to the saving activities of God. It did not listen to Saint Paul's reminder that the church "as a wild olive shoot" has been grafted in to share "the same root and sap of the olive tree"; the church does not sustain the root, but is sustained by the root (Rom. 11:17–18). Thus already by the time of Cyprian (d. 258) the theology of the new covenant was summed up in the dictum "Outside the church no salvation." A little later, the Christian community was even more caught up in the ambiguity of particularity which distorts all claims to universality. According to Saint Augustine, the virtues of the pagans are but "splendid vices." For centuries afterward, Christianity was unable to realize that where human life is being renewed and virtue expressed, the work of God is being actualized. It was even less able to admit that where human life is debased or destroyed, the work of God is being rejected, even when the best religious traditions, including those of Christianity, are being invoked. I will return to this tragic error in a moment.

The prophetic tradition in the Old Testament refused to identify the history of Israel as such with the totality of God's redeeming acts in the creation. It not only stressed that God's mission of redemption leads to a disruption of the history of a nation, organizing it into a history of salvation, but it also observed how deeply concerned God is about the fate of all peoples and how he assigns roles in his plan of salvation to certain nations. Already the story of Abraham being blessed by Melchizedek, king of Salem (Gen. 14:18–20), indicates that a blessing could flow from another nation to the people of Israel. According to Second Isaiah, Cyrus, king of Persia, a Gentile, who has no knowledge of the God of Israel, will carry out God's purpose and rebuild the holy city and the holy temple (Isa. 44:28): "For the sake of Jacob my servant and Israel my chosen I have called you [Cyrus] by name and given you your title, though you have not known me" (Isa. 45:4). The army of Nebuchadnezzar receives the land of Egypt as recompense, because the king of Babylon has worked for the Lord (Ezek. 29: 19–20). In the passage of Isaiah 19:21–25, Egypt is called "my people," Assyria "the work of my hands," and Israel "my possession." Israel does not stand out as a unique blessing to the world; rather in the company of Egypt and Assyria it receives blessings from God. Starting from faith in the sovereign God, the prophet Malachi is able to see the honest worship of nations being offered to the Lord:

From furthest east to furthest west my name is great among the nations. Everywhere fragrant sacrifice and pure gifts are offered in my name; for my name is great among the nations, says the Lord of Hosts (Mal. 1:11).

There is a direct link between these universalistic passages in the Old Testament and the unexpected and surprising universalistic perspective of Matthew 25:31–46: the Last Judgment of the Son of Man. Not Christians on the right side and "non-Christians" on the left side, but, according to the evangelist, all nations are summoned before his throne and separated into two groups. It is not stated that the Gospel has been proclaimed to all the world. The criterion for separation is rather baffling. There are not only righteous among those who have confessed his name and belong to his church but equally among those who have no consciousness of ever having served the Master. By the very spontaneity and unselfconsciousness of their love and their perseverance in well-doing, the righteous among all nations have proved themselves true sons and daughters of their heavenly Father. Those who pretended to know God and to have served him are cursed and not permitted to enter the kingdom. The Matthew passage contains a universalism which is, in the first place, inclusive and only then an exclusive universalism, something which has often been concealed and obscured in the presentation of the Christian message. At the last day Christ acknowledges as his own those people in all the world who have not known him but who have, without knowing it, served him in the person of their suffering neighbor. And Christ alone determines who has loved him and served his neighbor.

God's Acts in History Today and Tomorrow

It should be added here that the supreme Judge on the Last Day is the agonizing Christ. To this Christ we turned already in the preceding chapter. But this same vicariously suffering Christ is equally the sole key to the understanding of God's own plan of salvation, both in the Old and New Testaments and in the ongoing history of today and tomorrow. The parable in Matthew 25 neither simply describes those who are accepted nor does it offer any spur to conduct that can be morally achieved. If this is the case, only a few alarmingly self-righteous people within the nations would enjoy the kingdom. It is only in the light of the suffering Christ—and not on the basis of the western version of historical Christianity—that we can begin to see a profounder meaning of God's free dealing with many nations today, including the new China. The Chinese cannot be excluded from the sufferings of Jesus Christ who died in order that all men and women might become free to be human. They cannot be placed in the lump on his left hand side. What we have witnessed in the Great Leap Forward and the Great Proletarian Cultural Revolution is a painful struggle of the Chinese people to shake and to shape the present and the future of their nation. In their own view, they have still a long way to go before achieving certain goals. As we acknowledge these struggles, it is of no avail to downgrade the Chinese ideological thrust to a completely secularized version of salvation history. The suffering Christ makes no distinction between a "religious" and a "secular" mode of salvation. He is the incorporation of all the struggles of the poor, the underprivileged, and the dispossessed and does not put up with any kind of spiritualization of the Sermon on the Mount he preached to his contemporaries. The down-to-earth blessing of the poor is followed by an unequivocal condemnation of the rich. They will have had their time of happiness; they will go hungry and mourn and weep.

In the Calcuttas of this world we are still more driven back to the agony and death of Jesus Christ where we encounter the decisive saving act of God. It is in Christ's cross that we come to grips with the meaning of all human suffering and defeat. God's agony with the wrongs and evils that threaten to erode the foundation of his creation and at the same time his unchangeable love, pressing the disastrous course of human history toward a new creation, cannot be more profoundly expressed than in the crucifixion of his Son and in Calcutta. Salvation history is taking place every day in its slums and in its streets. For that reason world Christianity had better not continue benevolently acknowledging a possible salvation for those "who strive to live a good life without having arrived yet at an explicit knowledge of the saving God," even if such a sentence seems to update Christian theology. It is only in the sharing of God's unspeakable anguish for his creatures and in the wrestling with the hope of the hopeless that salvation can be proclaimed. That proclamation knows no limits excluding the whole of China and still less Calcutta. They are all part of the creation which, according to Romans 8:21, "will be set free from the bondage to decay and obtain the glorious liberty of the children of God."

From these few pages dealing with interpretations of salvation history another few conclusions can be drawn. As God's sovereign and inscrutable plan of salvation includes all peoples and all nations, the churches do not need to absolutize the value and the destiny of their particular community over against the value and destiny of other religious as well as secular communities. An open or hidden radical distinction cannot be made between the community of Christ-believers and communities of other-believers and nonbelievers since every final distinction has to be left entirely to God. In his kingdom there will not be first of all a Christian community and then perhaps also redeemed Muslim, Hindu, and Marxist communities but only *one* world community, in which he as the one God is ever present. Surely Calcutta will face the resurrected Christ bearing the marks of his crucifixion. The churches hope, founded on Matthew 25:31–46, that the kingdom of God will embody nations and peoples beyond their own expectation and understanding sets them free to search with others for new forms of human community, wherever and whenever possible. As the suffering Christ incessantly begs his followers to commit themselves to the task of finding human ways of living together, the defining of the true and unique nature of the church's fellowship cannot be undertaken as a distinctively separate task. The church responding to his calling is not a "pioneer" and "master of community initiative," but a humble and obedient servant. It therefore is not able to "sit back" and reflect on biblical terms and understandings of Christian community and communion without having the inclusive perspective of the kingdom of God always in mind.

In our times nothing less than the maturity and the truth of the Christian faith is at stake. As long as world Christianity thinks and behaves like God's predestined driving force of his *Heilsgeschichte*, the Christian faith bears the marks of immaturity, hypocrisy, and idolatry. It is in fact a false and inhuman faith which should not be propagated to an "unbelieving" world, even if it is nurtured by an impressive international crowd of millions of people. The faith in a suffering Lord does not need to be celebrated and defended by a multitude of churches against other religions and ideologies when precisely that suffering redeems every member of the human race. Christianity cannot think less of God and expect less of him than that he will save the whole world. The faith in a suffering Christ does not need to be made acceptable through many manifestations of Christian solidarity with the world when Christ himself liberates his followers from the delusion that the course of history depends on Christians and their permanent planning.

The systematic strengthening of the world Christian community vis-à-vis the "non-Christian" world is therefore out of place today because an authentic faith can only be concerned with the *whole* people of God. Being urged to search with other religious and nonreligious communities for a potential world community of communities, the churches remain immature as long as they wish to define still better and more precisely the nature of their own community. They are not grown up when they continue to question the desire of other communities to devote themselves to the quest of world community. Immature churches oscillate between still seeking a well-defined position in this world and being afraid of suffering the fate of powerlessness. Also specific ecumenical programs concerning human rights, world development, combating racism and so on, are consequently always in danger of being spurious, mere sideshows of the world Christian community, when they are not intimately related to the hopeless suffering of Jesus Christ. The churches' hesitation and fear to open themselves to other world communities is a clear sign that they have gravely underestimated the truly liberating power of their powerless Lord, crucified in the midst of this world.

Only a mature faith knows how to interpret the Sermon on the Mount and the Last Judgment of the Son of Man. These biblical passages do not apply to the end of world history but judge all Christian faith and action right now in our present time. In the light of these texts Christians are not allowed to speak so anxiously anymore of Christianity as the one absolute religion, of the pitfalls of syncretism, of the dangers of dialogue, and of the inevitable failure of human ideologies, as all these utterances can and do reflect a false Christian doctrine of humanity, of the church, of society, and of the kingdom of God. Matthew 5:1–10 and 25:31–46 do not conceive of world Christianity as the moving spirit in salvation history. They do not know the term "salvation history" at all but survey the whole of humankind divided into two parts, those to be rejected and those to be blessed. The criterion for judgment is the humanity of Christ, which has become transparent in the behavior of nations and individual human beings. Mature Christian faith therefore transcends present Christianity as it is solely concerned with the radiation of Christ's humanity in the entire human race. It does not speculate like theological seminaries, church headquarters, and ecumenical institutes which are running and are urging others to run in the right direction to obtain the crown of salvation. It stakes a claim that Calcutta is saved because God's love for his creation is most deeply rooted there, and there the righteous turn out to be the true sons and daughters of their heavenly Father.

Moral appeals and prophetic dramatizations will not help the churches to confess that they are not *per se* instruments of God's righteousness and not only alleviate but also aggravate the burdens and distresses of this world. The openness to other people's true humanity, the all-out search for a genuinely human community, and the joy that others are serving the Master, exceeding Christians in spontaneity and unselfconscious love, cannot be preached or recommended, not even to the best organized and most spirited Christian gatherings. This may sound strange and threatening. But it is true that the shape and the identity of the universal church will be found only by those who do not know that they are poor in spirit, meek, merciful, and pure in heart and continue to ask for a foretaste of world community and world communion which will be neither broken nor left unfulfilled.

8

TOWARD GREATER MATURITY

Since I chose as subtitle of his book "The Immaturity of World Christianity," I implicitly spoke at several places of the shortcomings and failures of Christianity and explicitly of immature churches being in need of a more mature faith and conduct on the last few pages of the foregoing chapter. I now would like to devote this last chapter to more direct questions of greater maturity of world Christianity and of how contemporary theology can stir up Christians and Christian communities and accompany them in the process of becoming less self-seeking, boastful, envious, suspicious, offended, specious, ambitious, and activistic, and more honest, receptive, generous, expectant, genuinely indignant, and truly responsible, or in a word, more fully mature. I do not use these adjectives in an exhortative and moral sense, but in the context of the Beatitudes and in connection with the spiritual gifts, described in 1 Corinthians 13.

Submitting three theses and expounding them to some extent, I hope that the reader will bear with the declaratory and shorthand nature of my propositions. I have tried to be concise, outlining the immediate future course of world Christianity and of the ecumenical movement, and the need of both to concentrate more on the heart of the Christian faith, on the most important issues and most crucial priorities, and the inner connection between them. In company with many fellow Christians I am convinced and hopeful that contemporary Christianity can attain a greater maturity and manifest a more inclusive hope with regard to the entire world, the course of humankind's history, and the delicate nature and transcending purpose of its own constituency.

I

Christian theology is basically a theology of the cross. The crucified Christ opens the dialogical relationship to God by revealing the Father's self-humiliation (Philippians 2) and his acceptance of humanity's destitution and forlornness. When Jesus cried: "My God, why hast thou forsaken me" and died, it was not his followers but the pagan centurion who replied: "Truly this man was the son of God" (Mark 15:35–39). Miserable and godless humanity is taken into full communion with God without any condition or limit. In order to grasp the meaning of Christ's suffering and death, the theology of the crucified God must be nourished and confirmed by a theology of the triune God. In the meeting with people of other faiths or no faith, however, the authenticity of a monotheistic concept of God (Judaism and Islam), a polytheistic concept of God (Hinduism), and an atheistic belief (Buddhism), and the conviction that God is a sheer projection out of humanity's helplessness (communism), can be deeply questioned only by a theology of a "God in pain" and a theology of a "God who lets himself be pushed out of the world on the cross." Christian theology of the cross penetrates into the terrifying mystery of individual and collective sin, only partially grasped, but on the whole ignored or rejected by all religions and ideologies.

Some Christians reflecting upon my critical evaluation of Christianity and the ecumenical movement throughout this book and upon the contents of this first thesis will undoubtedly object to my reductions and oversimplifications of a number of theological issues. They can easily accuse me of a new kind of patripassianism and binitarianism, both heretical doctrines of early centuries. The Father suffers and the Son suffers, but there is no mention of the Holy Spirit. Christ's godforsakenness is a necessary element but not the final word in God's plan of salvation. The "Comforter," they will assert, is the true source of hope in the final triumph of God and of his kingdom in creation. The doctrine of the Trinity, expressing the mutuality and reciprocity of indwelling whereby the love, which is God, passes and repasses among Father, Son, and Holy Spirit, must remain the pivot of Christianity on which everything hinges. Also the Basis of the World Council of Churches explicitly includes the trinitarian formula.

Others may object to what they will feel to be an overconfident and unfounded universalistic trend in this book. The doctrine of universalism shared by several early Greek Fathers and taught by a number of liberal theologians during the last century and a half, they will contend, is clearly refuted by the Bible. The "universal" statement of John 3:16, for instance, is restricted to "whosoever believes." Similarly, Saint Paul's conclusion that "one man died for all and therefore all mankind has died" (2 Cor. 5:14) does not refer to all men and women but to those who die in Christ. Christ's atonement is universal only in the sense that it is unconditionally *offered* to all human beings. The mystery of divine election cannot be overlooked. It is the supreme task of the church, they conclude, to declare faithfully God's mercy and love in his reconciling work in the dead and risen Christ.

In spite of the soundness and completeness of these arguments, I believe that Christian theology still does not adequately perform its task in the church for the sake of the world. Unless theology moves along the edge of patripassianism and universalism, it underestimates the saving power of the Gospel for Christians, affluent westerners, secular Russians, Chinese, and Calcutta street dwellers alike, and cannot communicate it to them. Christianity will reach a more mature stage only when the relation between the universality and complexity of sin and God's way of dealing with the wretchedness and destructiveness of that sin is more deeply fathomed. Similarly, Christianity will come of age only when it sails with fear and trembling between the Scylla of the church as the sign and seal of the kingdom and the Charybdis of Origen's idea of *Apocatastasis,* which openly allows for the hope that all free moral creatures, angels, human beings, and devils, will ultimately share in the grace of God's salvation. When God is said to be present and active everywhere in the whole world, he is nowhere. But when he is located only inside and not outside the "Christian world," it had better be confessed that the Holy Spirit is working and redeeming at all times in all religions and in all cultures.

I owe much to Canon David Jenkins who so articulately speaks in his book, *The Contradiction of Christianity,* of the "hopefulness of solidarity in sin," the "judgment from the poor and the excluded," and "obstacles to being human." "Unless sinfulness is recognized as something shared in by all human beings," he writes, "then there is no escape from the dehumanizing limitations of false and premature absolutes proclaimed by limited and partial agents of a partially understood historical process."[1] Christianity is not exempt from behaving as a "limited and partial agent." "Men and women," according to Canon Jenkins, "need to be liberated from the inhumanities of a Christianity and a Christendom which have played their part in distorting the future of the Kingdom into past and present tyrannies of moral and political ideologies and structures."[2] This is especially true when the intricate problem of the world's masses of exploited and poor is raised. Throughout this book I have argued that world Christianity has entered into a deadend street by promoting itself to a chief advocate of the Third and Fourth World, on the ground of an apparently healthy and relevant but in fact still deficient theology. David Jenkins still deepens my reflections when he writes that "the poor and the marginals are not primarily objects of charity and compassion but rather subjects and agents of the judgment of God and pointing to the ways of the Kingdom."[3]

This insight reinforces my thesis that faith in the triune God is based on the suffering and agonizing Christ who continues to suffer and to agonize until all human beings (including Christians) become human. Indeed, Christianity is always in danger of proclaiming premature and false absolutes and of distorting the future of the kingdom in their very acts of compassion and service. I have already pointed out in Chapter 6 of this book that the ecumenical movement is at present rather satisfied because it has found again a right balance between the vertical dimension of faith and the horizontal dimension of love, between evangelism and humanization, conversion of the heart and change of social structures. I can now add that mature Christianity knows that it still has to be liberated even from the idea of a dialectic between confession and commitment. It knows that it still has to be liberated from all good theology of liberation and all passionate struggles for liberation of the poor and the oppressed.

Maturer Christianity will pray that its relatively deep inspirations, its relatively good structures, and its relatively successful actions will be set free by Christ on the cross, who himself knows the abyss of human bondage and sustains our weak and sinful human efforts to obtain a greater freedom. It will also ardently pray that Buddhists,

Muslims, communists, and all others will discover their imprison-
ment in the same human labyrinth of apostasy and rebellion against
God, and that, as in the case of the pagan Roman officer, the scales
will also from their eyes fall when the exhausted Christ reveals his
godforsakenness. Christians everywhere will not be afraid to point
to their own captivity in sin, to their boast of knowing better and
performing better than fellow human beings, and to their inclination
to detect the disastrous gaps and errors in other religions and
ideologies, instead of proclaiming the crucified God as the center of
the Gospel. Living in the hopefulness of solidarity in sin and experiencing that God the disturber of both the rich and the poor and
the crucified God are one and the same God, they will no longer
need to pretend. They will repeat as the eyewitnesses of Christ's
execution that this man has the power to liberate all men and
women. This leads me to my second thesis.

II

*Christian theology is basically dialogical theology. It catches glimpses of
God's incredible truth and communicates that truth in living in community with people of other religions and ideologies. The center of world
Christianity is to be found at its unexplored and unprotected frontiers,
because its truth is universal and accessible to all human beings without
any preliminary knowledge of God incarnate in Jesus Christ. Christian
dialogical theology collects the stories of how and why other believers and
nonbelievers reject or accept Jesus Christ and interprets these stories to the
Christian community. Christian concepts of society are valid and viable
only when conceived and put into practice in dialogical relationships.*

Several times, perhaps even *ad nauseam,* I have pointed out that
many intelligent and animated gatherings discussing the nature and
strategy of mission and evangelism are only too frequently a waste of
time and energy. As librarian and archivist of the World Council of
Churches in Geneva I cannot think and react otherwise, since I very
frequently have to survey the hundreds of conferences which have
taken place in the three realms of Faith and Order, World Mission
and Evangelism, and Church and Society during this century.
Thousands of Christians have participated in these endless conferences, and thousands of Christians have sought new inspiration,

hammered out new policies and tactics, and pledged new commitment. Being drawn into the many intricacies and fascinations of all these and other gatherings, Christians always seem to lose sight of the process whereby people discover their own salvation. So far very little indeed has been reported on how people are actually drawn into communion with Christ. The missionary avant-garde has in fact not much to say on Hindu, Marxist, and Muslim discipleship of Jesus Christ, as it cannot report on the long, delicate, and often fatiguing process of testifying to the God in inconceivable pain and incorporating a small part of that pain into one's own daily life. It therefore does not realize that there is a great difference between pressing others to accept membership in one or another denominational church—this can still be labelled spiritual domination and institutional manipulation—and reminding fellow men and women of their right to reach out to an ultimate hope without necessarily betraying their loyalty to their own community. How difficult it is for Christianity to realize that the task of being "ambassadors of reconciliation" would be an impossible one if Christ's kingdom were not already present today in the outspoken "non-Christian" world.

For maturer world Christianity both mission and evangelism are no longer the same old and intricate problems as before. Its campaigning for submission to Christ no longer aims at the conversion of Hindus who are ready to make a complete break with their gods and goddesses, their caste system, their natural inclination to pantheism, and their Indian mysticism. Christian mission no longer wishes to save souls for Christ when these souls cannot take wings from their ancient culture and natural community into a threatening alien culture and an unfamiliar new community (the denominational-minded church). World evangelism no longer rejoices when Hindus are converted *from* their polytheist religion, but it rejoices when they claim to belong *to* the communion of all believers in Christ, without living in conflict and tension with their rich Hindu past and disavowing their Hindu community. Hindu Christians are spiritually better equipped to deal with the prejudices and suspicions of their fellow Hindus and can be better ambassadors for Christ when they compare the farfetched hope of an *ultimate* synthesis of the universal holy power (*Brahman*) and the eternal self (*atman*) with the sudden joy over the reconciliation of the still divinely suffering God with his suffering creatures *today*.

When it one day re-enters China, mature Christianity will not forget that the Christian missions failed to understand two basic components in Chinese culture: namely, a pervasive and many-faceted naturalism and the profound and rich humanism of the Confucian tradition. It will remember that the social irrelevance of missionary societies prevented the Chinese from creating their own indigenous and authentic framework for the Gospel. When meeting the Chinese communists face to face, world Christianity will not present its long catalogue of queries and objections to their coercive, monolithic, and atheistic society, but will dare to say that the Father will bless those who gave the hungry food, gave the thirsty to drink, and clothed the naked. Only then will it perhaps have a chance to interrogate the Chinese people on the meaning of our individual suffering and death and on the honesty and integrity of the communist party not manipulating the masses for its own preposterous and inhuman ends. Only then will it perhaps be able to point out that the power to remove landlords and mandarins from their thrones, to lift up the poor, and to build a new society without want is indeed a great but not the greatest power, as even the most effective liberation from oppressive structures cannot guarantee full humanity. The wholeness of humanity, Christians will confess, is assured only by the suffering power of Jesus Christ.

World Christianity, which has come of age, will no longer set about clarifying the relation among dialogue, mission, and witness in "internal dialogues" among Christians. When faced with other religions and ideological communities, instead of initiating ever new processes of theological reflection on why, how, and where the church should seek community with these communities and proclaim Christ conclusively, it will collect the many stories of Christians who live with Marxists, Jews, Muslims, and Hindus who share their frustrations and hopes, and who wait for precious moments when curious questions about the origin and nature of their faith are asked. Much depends on their attitude and behavior inspiring confidence and impelling the partners to engage in a more intensive conversation.

Christians will try to explain, often only with stammering words, why the suffering Christ has become the center of their life and how they are awaiting the ever approaching kingdom in which God himself will wipe the tears from many eyes. They will add that their interlocutors are as much a part of that kingdom as they themselves. Having collected a great number of such personal narratives, missionaries will then report to their fellow Christians who have no experience of living in community with people of other faiths and no faith—still a vast majority of Christians have dialogued only on the expediency of dialogue. Then the relation between dialogue, mission, and witness can be discussed in a greater depth, strengthening the unity of the Christian community and recruiting more rather amateurish and inarticulate—but precisely for that reason reliable— messengers of God's love in Jesus Christ. Then also the pastoral concern for those who still feel threatened by "hazards" of dialogue and are still marked by the fear of syncretism will no longer be out of place.

In the light of the second thesis no further attempt will be made to arrive at a valid and widely applicable Christian concept of society without inviting intensive participation of "non-Christians." M. M. Thomas, the former chairman of the World Council of Churches Central Committee, recently wrote:

Charles Raven has reminded us that *koinonia,* the word for fellowship, has three meanings: Community, Communion and Communism. All the three are relevant goals not only for the Church but also for secular society.

Of these Raven says: "We have tried to escape the third; it's time we realized that it is inherent in the other two and in the word itself." The former Chairman concludes:

The idea of a "Christ-centered secular ecumenism" or of "a secular fellowship in Christ" has come to the forefront of Christian thinking today. . . . The secular human fellowship informed by Christ should struggle to achieve, not merely inter-personal relations of love, but also structures of communitarian social living.[4]

It is quite clear that if one speaks of a secular fellowship in Christ, that this fellowship can be real only if the churches and their faithful conceive—together with secular governments, political parties, and ideological pressure groups—of a new society, and then struggle side by side to approximate that new society. Separate formulation of ideological concepts and separate commitments to put these concepts into practice make of the secular fellowship in Christ a mockery. The idea of the "just, participatory, and sustainable society" will therefore be severely criticized on the grounds that it is promoted exclusively by Christians—whether they live in East and West, North and South makes no difference—and by some others who are on the fringe of the world Christian community. Besides the fact that the idea is "undialogical," it will also be criticized for the eschatological reason that it lacks an utter concern for the more than blighted future of impoverished and overpopulated nations. I will return to this point in a moment. Last but not least, the idea of a just and sustainable society will be called into question because humanization (based on the suffering and death of Jesus Christ) is for the neocapitalist consolidation of society an unintended by-product, as the necessity of solidarity is accidental, while for socialist ideologies humanization is an explicit goal and a common vital struggle. Since it is true that *koinonia* implies communism, world Christianity that continues to define the structures and conditions of this fellowship on its own terms will only become more unecumenical and more sectarian.

III

Christian theology is basically an eschatologically orientated theology. It constantly reminds the universal church that it will not be freed from its shackles of subtle activism, subtle moralism, and subtle discrimination unless it accepts that the old is, above all, anticipation replaced by the new and not by its past, and God's future conditions the present. Eschatological theology "thrives" on the inexplicable tension between the kingdom of God, which will totally transform human relations in society, and the unverifiable contributions of many people (not only Christians) to that kingdom (Matt. 25). Whenever and wherever this tension is only slightly reduced, Christianity is in great danger of falling a victim to a neo-Social Gospel, which in spite of its sophistication and applicability is as adolescent and vulnerable as the original Social Gospel.

As is well known, the Social Gospel movement had wide influence on American, and partly also European, Protestantism from about 1890 to the 1930s. Its leading spokesman was an American Baptist minister, Walter Rauschenbusch (1861–1918), who was of the opinion that individual human beings will not be redeemed unless society is redeemed. The essential demand of the Social Gospel was a social order reflecting the fatherhood of God and the brotherhood of men. Other characteristics of this widespread movement were belief in the essential goodness of people and their responsiveness to moral suasion (sin is primarily selfishness), stress on the immanence and nearness of God (though his transcendence was not denied) and the undelayed arrival of the kingdom of God as the center of Jesus' message, and the belief that through self-sacrifice and determined individual and corporate efforts Christians can become heroes of the coming dawn. Although the Social Gospel was sensitive to the fact of the corporate transmission of sin through human institutions, it was convinced that social salvation would come as institutions as well as individuals are brought under the law of love.

Christianity today does not share the oversimple belief in the essential goodness of humanity, in its ability to make the right choices and so to contribute to the ushering in of the kingdom. Far more keenly aware of the magnitude and complexity of sociopolitical problems it focuses less on individual motivation and individualistic action in society, and more on analyzing and collectively combatting structural and institutional injustice. Also in the ecumenical movement considerable progress has been made in encouraging the churches to re-examine their traditional status quo positions on political tensions, social and economic conflicts, and explosive international affairs. The churches are constantly stimulated to clearer thinking and more courageous action in solidarity with those who struggle to change unjust and oppressive infrastructures. They are also urged to liberate themselves from their captivity to the prevailing power structures.

Yet in spite of a more sober and realistic approach to the numerous political and socio-economic problems of human societies, and in spite of a deeper consciousness of the unbridgeable gulf between the righteousness of the kingdom and the righteousness of empirical societies, world Christianity seems to be caught in a neo-Social Gospel, which carries the same traits (an activist emphasis and a passionate concern for justice) as the Social Gospel movement. I do not agree with contemporary theologians that the Christian message today is in danger of being reduced to a certain purely secular social-ethical program, which is merely absorbed by socio-political programs. The problem is not that the church, on the one hand, has been politicized and, on the other hand, is unable to reiterate that the religious and transcendental roots of the Christian revelation in matters of social action are significant. The real problem is that the church, having entered an overactivist phase, is so preoccupied with pointing to patterns of exploitation and domination and with organizing programs supporting the underprivileged, victims of human rights violations, the underdeveloped, and the racially oppressed, that it not only *assists* peoples and nations in their struggles for liberation but becomes an insider, promoter, and administrator of God's scheme of salvation. The word "assistance" not only suggests a paternalistic and watchful attitude but also underlines the churches' vital role of laboring for a new humanity. World Christianity fails to acknowledge that if the peoples' and nations' struggles for liberation and a more abundant life are not at least as much as the church's activities a part of Christ's endless struggling, then he agonizes and labors in vain.

It was not accidental that I started this book by referring to the continuation of conventional Christianity and the power of ecclesiastical establishments. I hope that by now it has become even clearer that the prevailing form of Gross National Product (GNP) Christianity expresses as much a denominationally structured and bureaucratically corporate consciousness as it breeds various forms of sophisticated works-righteousness and immature notions of historical progress, even if this progress is not seen as automatic or inevitable but conditional upon the Christian's response to divine leading. GNP Christianity and the neo-Social Gospel belong together and condition one another. Statistics of achievements, not qualitative judgments, serve as the basis for evaluation of the effectiveness of the churches' actions. A burden of unreal guilt is heaped upon members of churches whose statistics lag behind the quantitative data of other denominations. The naive judgment that quantity of commitment reflects quality of commitment remains at the heart of GNP Christianity. But still worse: the programs and actions of the GNP church are given "ontological and permanent" status, while in fact they can only have an "enabling, initiating and entrepreneurial character." There is no clear insight that truly representative "Christian programs" are of an ideological nature and have to be worked out in the "secular fellowship of Christ," in which all citizens, governments, and parties share the responsibility of doing God's will and struggling (ideologically) together against principalities and powers until the Lord himself will ultimately reign over a divided humanity.

Mature Christianity recaptures the vision and hope of a radical and total transformation of all human institutions, all human relations, and all human ambitions. In the kingdom of God not only every individual and institutional alienation will be done away with, but religious answers to secular questions will become superfluous. The distinction between sacred and secular will be abolished. There will be neither a new temple nor another struggle for human liberation. Reminding contemporary ideologies, and in particular various forms of Marxism, that alienation in society can never be completely overcome, mature Christianity will add that for that reason alone religion is a penultimate but not an ultimate necessity in this human life. It is a necessity only insofar as religion must provide answers to secular questions until these answers are no longer religious answers at all, that is to say, until the real sources of human alienation are overcome. Karl Marx was right when he wrote:

The religious reflex of the real world can, in any case, only then vanish when the practical relations of everyday life offer to man none but perfectly intelligible and reasonable relations with regard to his fellowmen and to nature.[5]

This statement puts contemporary Christians to shame since they do not speak enough of Christ as the new human being, since they testify too seldom to the Holy Spirit as the liberating power of a future that is open, and since they even less frequently bear witness to that universal reign of God when Christ shall once more be subordinate to the Father, when all men and women shall be free, when all nations shall be reconciled, and when God will be all in all (Isa. 49:6; 1 Cor. 15:28). This witness could find open ears among communists as they are right to insist that secular concerns already now matter far more than religious ones. Their blindness and only capital mistake is still to believe that "perfectly intelligible and reasonable relations" will be established through indefatigable and strong human efforts. But immature Christians commit several grave mistakes. They are wrong to insist that the Christian religion has an ultimate function in human life. They are in error in believing that joint Christian endeavors are of a particular religious significance to the world and should be imitated by all "non-Christians." Their greatest shortcoming, however, is to be unable to relate secular social struggles and ideological controversies to the coming of the kingdom, which is the fulfillment, not of Christian social ethics, but of humankind's laboring and groaning for a better world, including the church's laboring and groaning for that world.

Is it at all possible, one is inclined to ask, to cultivate a whole new Christian ethic that not only would amount to a transvaluation of the values of the Christian GNP system but also to a worldwide understanding in greater depth of the consequences and conclusions to be drawn from Matthew 25:31–46? I have one immediate suggestion to make. Perhaps the "justice and service" units of the World Council of Churches, of many regional and national ecumenical organizations, and the boards for social responsibility, social work, and social services of national denominations should call a three-year halt to their activities, except for emergency charitable and rescuing services. During this period a much wider study and deeper concentration on what I so brokenly and stutteringly outlined in this last chapter could take place. Intensive group reflection should lead to a far more careful use of the new term "spirituality for combat," coined by David Jenkins and used by M. M. Thomas at the World Council's Assembly in Nairobi in 1975,[6] for that term can wrongly suggest that a specific Christian spirituality is needed for right combat and any meaningful and successful combat originates from and depends upon the right Christian spirituality. When the churches, supported by a "theology and spirituality for combat," have an opportunity "to speak to mankind at large," it remains to be seen whether their voice is really prophetic and not just opinionated, parochial, and self-sufficient.

A considerable amount of money would become available and could be invested for that same period in the "faith and witness" and "education and renewal" units of the same Christian institutions and organizations. Their task would not be as before *to reflect* on issues of a more visible unity of the church, a widening conciliar fellowship, an intelligible confessing of Jesus' name today, a daily practice of spirituality, and corresponding new styles of life, but to seek for *working models* of these concerns and *to practice* them in many churches and congregations which are deeply concerned about their identity and an authentic place in this world. The important matter of Christian communities in mission and dialogue would gain a whole new impetus. A deeper awareness would arise that ecumenical affairs of church union, witness, church and society, education and dialogue, and their corresponding service programs are all inter-related and essential parts of the total twentieth-century ecumenical movement and its all-encompassing hope. I do not make this sugges-tion because I have been "converted" to a "conservative evangelical" stand or attracted to the hidden power of Eastern Orthodox spiritu-ality but because I cannot but anticipate the surprise of being asked to enter with others, who seemed to be "non-Christians," into the kingdom of God. Mature Christianity radiates this waiting for sur-prise and the free sharing with others in unexpected salvation.

This leads me to my last point. It has very likely been noted that the church itself, its inner life, and its manifestations are absent in the three main theses. There is no reference to the necessity of up-dating the doctrine of the church. The theology of the cross, the theology of dialogue, and the strong emphasis on eschatology, my critics can object, have relegated ecclesiology into the background of serious consideration. This way of arguing for a separate and special treatment of the church mirrors, I am afraid, a typically im-mature Christian theology. A proper understanding of the church cannot start with the church itself, but must be related to the king-dom of God and the final destination of human history. It is in fact quite possible and feasible to conceive of the kingdom without any church at all. But as we have seen, the coming kingdom is not an otherworldly phenomenon, but the destiny of present political and ideological society; thus the critical and constructive role of the church as an eschatological community is to encourage governments and political parties to assume their responsibilities, to inspire their visions of social actions. In doing so the church affirms that the future of the kingdom releases a dynamic in the present which kindles peoples' dreams of a truly human community and gives meaning to their fervent quest for political forms of justice and love.

Only then is it in a position to remind nations and states that all new models of society, in contrast with the ultimacy of God's kingdom, will always turn out to be preliminary and provisional. If the Christian eschatological community does not perform this encouraging and critical function, it remains either a religious institution catering to the religious needs of those who unhesitatingly identify the church with the "spiritual" kingdom, or an ecclesiastical organization providing its members, who believe that the church is the present form of the kingdom—only in time to be distinguished from the kingdom's future fulfillment—with a good conscience to be in the forefront of the struggle for a more human society, a struggle which cannot be matched by secular institutions. Whether occupied with unique spiritual and otherworldly matters or with a unique involvement in social matters, the church is then in every respect not more than an association of common religious interests with a disdain for false religious and atheistic endeavors to change conditions of humans living together.

There is still another side to the question of how to arrive at a more mature and credible conception of the church. It is Prof. José Míguez Bonino, Dean of Postgraduate Studies of the Higher Evangelical Institute for Theological Studies in Buenos Aires and a President of the World Council of Churches, I believe, who has prepared some ground for an up-to-date ecclesiology. In the last chapter of his book *Doing Theology in a Revolutionary Situation* he ascertains that the ecclesiologies of the Reformation and the Counter-Reformation are in a deep crisis:

In a predominantly static, intellectualistic and juridically minded frame of reference, the criteria adopted (for these old and even more recent ecclesiologies) were backward-looking (historical, institutional, or demonstrable continuity with the past).[7]

Very similarly, as I just inferred, Míguez Bonino believes that the eschatological vocation of the church, its call to witness to the coming kingdom, must take precedence over a static identity with its origin. He is not afraid to state that today "an untidy ecclesiological situation is the necessary expression of an untidy ecclesial situation and we should not strive to overcome it artificially."[8]

His whole argument for a fluid and academically not definable form of the Christian community centers around the insight that the poor in all the world are constitutive of the mystery of the church. This proposition can be accepted only by avoiding two basic mistakes. On the one hand, it can all too quickly be overemphasized that Christians are in solidarity with the poor and struggle for the liberation of the poor. Such a statement is a half-truth and smacks of a neopaternalism. On the other hand, the poor themselves are not actively working for the liberation of comfortable Christians and the salvation of the bourgeois church. If nonbelieving revolutionaries among the exploited are baptized potential, crypto, or unwitting Christians, again a new form of Christian paternalistic condescendence becomes apparent. To say that the poor are constitutive of the mystery of the church is to repeat that the church is where Christ is. But Christ is where the poor are. He utterly identifies himself with oppressed, destitute, and abandoned human beings. In his death the church meets the powerless, suffering, godforsaken human being as the last reality of God himself. The Christ struggling for the poor is the permanent disturber of the organization, liturgy, and forms of teaching of the church, which can and do become factors of oppression and alienation that operate as a part of the religous life itself. The same Christ, representing the destitute and abandoned, shatters all false optimism that ecclesiastical ingenuity and religious power will not become bankrupt when God is conceived as a protective assurance against exploitation, destitution, and death. In terms of Christian action, this means that the poor are not an external entity to which the church relates but an integral and structuring part of the whole community of faith. "Christ is present in the believer through faith," Míguez Bonino says, "and in the poor according to his promise." And he continues:

The whole doctrine of the Church must be thought out between these two poles which question each other. The depth of the Church's alienation is plumbed by the fact that these two faces of the Church are separated from each other and in mutual opposition—the community of faith has become predominantly the Church of the rich and the powerful and consequently the poor have been alienated from an explicit recognition of the Christ.[9]

Dietrich Bonhoeffer's main contribution to modern theology has been his "discoveries" of the world come of age, the religionless interpretation of Christianity, and the secret discipline *(Arkan-disziplin)*. This last notion implied for the German theologian that the inner life of the Christian community must become, as in the early period of the church, a "silent and hidden affair," and not remain a massive manifestation of its endurance, unity, and glory. The centuries-old pattern, wherein the church sought to adorn its Lord by embellishing and displaying publicly its corporate life, should be abandoned in the modern secular world. The idea of the secret discipline is intimately related to the concern for the world come of age—not the world performing better than the church but, at least as much as the church, entitled to its own initiative and autonomy. It is also related to the concern for the religionless interpretation of Christianity. It starts its task by taking utterly seriously atheism's claim that God is in no way a demanding and all-absorbing contemporary human possibility. This idea of the secret discipline sheds still more light on the urgency of spelling out a new provisional ecumenical ecclesiology.

Not only the poor and the marginals are alienated from the church but also many more millions of people to whom various ideologies of Marxism-Leninism constantly communicate that the powers and the possibilities of human beings are whatever they make them to be. Bonhoeffer has understood that the glory of God and the glory of the church demand and authorize the most ruthless and rigorous engagement with all secular realities in their own proper autonomy, authority, and hardness. Only then will Christians be able to situate truly anew the church in the midst of the world and to celebrate in their hidden sanctuary—yet for all others outside that sanctuary—that Jesus is the historical embodiment of a fusion of the glory of God and a passion for people, in other words, that God does embrace and define all reality.

The secret discipline obliges the Roman Catholic church, the World Council of Churches, and other Christian communities to change their powerful and massive systems of communication. At the beginning of this book I referred to the fabulous annual output of Christian books, pamphlets, and periodicals all over the world. It is precisely the rediscovery of the centrality of the cross, the readiness to engage in genuine dialogues, and a new living in a profound eschatological perspective that will prevent, I believe, the worldwide Christian community from circulating its literature that is apparently pastoral, normative, and authentic, but in fact is propagandistic, monological, and euphemistic. People of other faiths, abhorring the idea of a "crucified God," and people of no faith, excited about Marx's insight that "man must now revolve about himself as his own true sun," will prick up their ears and perhaps catch a glimpse of the deep humanness and humaneness of the Christian faith only when official churches and individual Christians alike can testify both to their strength and weakness, their advance and defeat, their hope and disillusionment. Unless a greater self-criticism and repentance is exercised and a greater modesty and self-denial explicitly manifested, the immaturity of a Christianity that claims always to be on the right side and in good business will become even more obvious.

It was not by accident that Bonhoeffer observed in his short life that it is frequently more natural and much easier to introduce the name of Christ to professed unbelievers than to Christian neighbors. Indeed, the *Arkandisziplin* leads out of the church and out of religious longing into the fellowship of unbelievers and other believers. And only by being with the godless and the oppressed is it possible to redefine the very peculiar nature of the church. There is much seemingly wise Christian talk that the church is in this world but not of this world. This affirmation confirms the fact that the church in practice is all too frequently neither truly in this world nor truly not of this world. The notion of the secret discipline corrects the falsehood of the statement because it puts all emphasis on the Christian community being *in* this world and thus by God's immeasurable grace not *of* this world.

The pertinent new insights of the theologians I just mentioned need to be developed much further, and I myself should have dwelt much longer on them. My intention here was only to introduce them and to indicate in which direction maturer Christianity can and will move. Christianity tomorrow will be able to bear with a fluctuating (powerless) and an ambiguous (suffering) church because it seeks to be identified with God's son on the cross who is the "dialoguer" par excellence between the rich and the poor, between believers and unbelievers, drawing both his disciples and those who serve him but say they do not know him into the wake of his ever approaching kingdom. Mature Christendom rediscovers that in the Sermon on the Mount no reference is made to people who properly define the church, devoutly worship, discuss the missionary structure of the congregation, reconceive the right relationship between the church and the world, and collect and invest large sums of money in significant church programs, but to people who are pure in heart, hunger and thirst for righteousness, and make peace. In the language of our times one could say that the Sermon speaks of people who search for the crucified Christ in China and Calcutta pleading with its populations to discover with them this same Christ. The Sermon also calls blessed those who know that the political and ideological struggles of this world require still more commitment and involvement than the promotion of international and national Christian goals. The people of the Beatitudes, of course, also worship, but differently from traditional Christian churches, because their identity is not ecumenically fragmented (in terms of the inhabited versus the uninhabited world) but dialogically and eschatologically whole. They daily celebrate God's promise for a redeemed, glorified, and united creation and cannot wait until all the world will share in that celebration.

NOTES

Chapter 1

1. W. H. van de Pol, *The End of Conventional Christianity* (New York: Newman Press, 1968), p. 15.

2. Ibid., p. 297.

3. Ibid., p. 14.

4. Corrado Pallenberg, *Vatican Finances* (Harmondsworth, Eng.: Pelican Books, 1973), pp. 154–55.

5. Alfred Balk, *The Religion Business* (Richmond, Va.: John Knox Press, 1968), pp. 5 and 8.

Chapter 2

1. "Minutes and Reports of the Fourth Meeting of the Central Committee, Rolle (Switzerland), August 4–11, 1951" (Geneva: World Council of Churches, 1951), p. 65.

2. "Minutes and Reports of the Twenty-Fourth Meeting of the Central Committee, Addis Ababa, January 10–21, 1971" (Geneva: World Council of Churches, 1971), pp. 165–66.

3. David M. Paton, ed., *Breaking Barriers, Nairobi 1975* (London: SPCK and Grand Rapids, Mich.: Wm. B. Eerdmans Publishing Company, 1976), p. 318.

4. *The Uppsala Report* (Geneva: World Council of Churches, 1968), p. 17.

5. David M. Paton, ed., *Breaking Barriers, Nairobi 1975*, p. 60.

6. *The New Delhi Report* (London: SCM, 1962), p. 426.

Chapter 3

1. "Minutes and Reports of the Twenty-Fourth Meeting of the Central Committee, Addis Ababa, 1971," pp. 130–33.

2. The sentence was used in a slide-tape presentation and later printed on a poster.

3. W. A. Visser't Hooft, *No Other Name: The Choice Between Syncretism and Christian Universalism* (London: SCM, 1963), p. 116.

4. Ibid., p. 124.

5. Ibid., p. 122.

6. Ibid., p. 118.

7. S. J. Samartha, ed., *Living Faiths and the Ecumenical Movement* (Geneva: World Council of Churches, 1971), p. 23.

8. W. C. Smith, *The Meaning and End of Religion* (New York: Macmillan, 1962), p. 11.

Chapter 4

1. S. J. Samartha, ed., *Living Faiths and the Ecumenical Movement*, p. 35.

2. P. S. Minear, *Images of the Church in the New Testament* (Philadelphia: Westminster Press, 1960), p. 266.

3. David M. Paton, ed., *Breaking Barriers, Nairobi 1975*, p. 80.

4. S. J. Samartha, ed., *Towards World Community: The Colombo Papers* (Geneva: World Council of Churches, 1975), pp. 127–28.

Chapter 5

1. *The Churches Survey Their Task: Report of the Conference at Oxford, July 1937, on Church, Community and State* (London: Allen & Unwin, 1937).

2. *The World Mission of the Church: Tambaram, Madras, December 12–29, 1938* (London: International Missionary Council, 1939), p. 22.

3. Pius XI, *Divini Redemptoris* (New York: Paulist Press, 1937), pp. 4 and 26.

4. W. A. Visser't Hooft, ed., *The First Assembly of the World Council of Churches at Amsterdam, August 22–September 4, 1948* (London: SCM, 1949), p. 50.

5. *World Conference on Church and Society, Geneva, July 12–26, 1966* (Geneva: World Council of Churches, 1967), p. 202.

6. D. M. Gill, ed., *From Here to Where: Technology, Faith and the Future of Man* (Geneva: World Council of Churches, 1970), p. 76.

7. *World Conference on Church and Society, Geneva, July 12–26, 1966*, p. 206.

8. *Minutes of the Twenty-Seventh Meeting of the Central Committee, Berlin (West), August 11–18, 1974* (Geneva: World Council of Churches), pp. 31–32.

9. *Study Encounter* 11, no. 4 (1975): 1–2.

10. *L' homme chrétien et l'homme marxiste* (Paris: La Palatine, 1965), pp. 28 and 30.

11. P. Verghese, "EACC Assembly: Christian Action in the Asian Struggle" *Christian Century,* August 29, 1973, pp. 831–32.

12. David M. Paton, ed., *Breaking Barriers, Nairobi 1975,* pp. 104, 105, and 123.

13. *Anticipation* (Geneva: World Council of Churches), no. 19, November 1974, pp. 12–13.

14. David M. Paton, ed., *Breaking Barriers, Nairobi 1975,* p. 128.

15. *New York Times,* October 7, 1974.

16. *Minutes and Reports of the Central Committee, Utrecht, August 13–23, 1972* (Geneva: World Council of Churches, 1972), p. 173.

17. Hosea Williams, Press Release, Atlanta, Georgia, October 29, 1971.

Chapter 6

1. *Minutes and Reports of the Central Committee, Geneva August 22–29, 1973* (Geneva: World Council of Churches, 1973), p. 149.

2. K. Kitamori, *Theology of the Pain of God* (Richmond, Va.: John Knox Press, 1965), pp. 40, 35, 39, 23.

3. Dietrich Bonhoeffer, *Letters and Papers from Prison* (London: SCM, 1971), p. 360.

4. Jürgen Moltmann, *The Crucified God* (London: SCM, 1974), pp. 4, 39, 40.

5. *The Humanum Studies: A Collection of Documents* (Geneva: World Council of Churches, 1975), pp. 109–10.

Chapter 7

1. V. Hayward, *Christians and China* (Belfast: Christian Journals, 1974), p. 119.

Chapter 8

1. David E. Jenkins, *The Contradiction of Christianity* (London: SCM, 1976), p. 69.

2. Ibid., p. 96.

3. Ibid., p. 49.

4. M. M. Thomas, *Man and the Universe of Faith* (Madras: Christian Literature Society, 1975), pp. 139–41.

5. Karl Marx, *Capital* (London, 1930), 1:53–54.

6. David M. Paton, ed., *Breaking Barriers. Nairobi 1975.* pp. 237 and 240.

7. José Míguez Bonino, *Doing Theology in a Revolutionary Situation* (Philadelphia: Fortress Press, 1975), p. 155.

8. Ibid., p. 96.

9. Ibid., p. 160.